The PRISON EPISTLES:

PHILIPPIANS, EPHESIANS, COLOSSIANS, PHILEMON

by Fr. Lawrence R. Farley

CONCILIAR
PRESS
Chesterton, Indiana

THE PRISON EPISTLES:
PHILIPPIANS, EPHESIANS, COLOSSIANS, PHILEMON
© Copyright 2003 by Lawrence Farley

one volume of *The Orthodox Bible Study Companion* Series

All Rights Reserved

Published by   Conciliar Press
                  (A division of Conciliar Media Ministries)
                  P.O. Box 748
                  Chesterton, IN 46304

Printed in the United States of America

ISBN 978-1-888212-52-5

Dedicated to my parents,
Rheal and Vera,
who loved me into life

Table of Contents and Outline

The Epistle of St. Paul the Apostle to the Colossians

The Epistle of St. Paul the Apostle to Philemon

❧ Introduction ❧

A Word About Scholarship and Translation

This commentary was written for your grandmother. And for your plumber, your banker, your next-door neighbor, and the girl who serves you French fries at the nearby McDonald's. That is, it was written for the average layman, for the nonprofessional who feels a bit intimidated by the presence of copious footnotes, long bibliographies, and all those other things which so enrich the lives of academics. It is written for the pious Orthodox layman who is mystified by such things as Source Criticism, but who nonetheless wants to know what the Scriptures mean.

Therefore, it is unlike many other commentaries, which are written as contributions to the ongoing endeavor of scholarship and as parts of a continuous dialogue among scholars. That endeavor and dialogue is indeed worthwhile, but the present commentary forms no part of it. For it assumes, without argument, a certain point of view, and asserts it without defense, believing it to be consistent with the presuppositions of the Fathers and therefore consistent with Orthodox Tradition. It has but one aim: to be the sort of book a busy parish priest might put in the hands of an interested parishioner who says to him over coffee hour after Liturgy, "Father, I'm not sure I really get what St. Paul is saying in the Epistles. What does it all mean?" This commentary tries to tell the perplexed parishioner what the writers of the New Testament mean.

Regarding the translation used herein, an Italian proverb says, "All translators are traitors." (The proverb proves its own point, for it sounds better in Italian!) The point of the proverb, of course, is that no translation, however careful, can bring out all the nuances and meanings of the original, since no language can be the mathematical equivalent of another. The English translator is faced, it would seem, with a choice: either he can make the translation something of a rough paraphrase of the original and render it into flowing sonorous English; or he can attempt to make a fairly literal, word-for-word translation from the original with the resultant English being stilted, wooden, and clumsy.

These two basic and different approaches to translation correspond to two basic and different activities in the Church. The Church needs a translation of the Scriptures for use in worship. This should be in good, grammatical, and flowing English, as elegant as possible and suited to its function in the majestic worship of the Liturgy. The Church also needs a translation of the Scriptures for private study and for group Bible study. Here the elegance of its English is of lesser concern. What is of greater concern here is the bringing out of all the nuances found in the original. Thus this approach will tend to sacrifice elegance for literality and, wherever possible, seek a word-for-word correspondence with the Greek. Also, because the student will want to see how the biblical authors use a particular word (especially St. Paul, who has many works included in the canon), a consistency of translation will be sought and the same Greek word will be translated, wherever possible, by the same English word or by its cognate.

The present work does not pretend to be anything other than a translation for private Bible study. It seeks to achieve, as much as possible, a literal, word-for-word correspondence with the Greek. The aim has been to present a translation from which one could jump back into the Greek original with the aid of an interlinear New Testament. Where a single Greek word has been used in the original, I have tried to find (or invent!) a single English word.

The result, of course, is a translation so literally rendered from the Greek that it represents an English spoken nowhere on the planet! That is, it represents a kind of "study Bible English" and not an actual vernacular. It was never intended for use outside the present commentaries, much less in the worship of the Church. The task of producing a flowing, elegant translation that nonetheless preserves the integrity and nuances of the original I cheerfully leave to hands more competent than mine.

The Prison Epistles

St. Paul's arrival in Rome was perhaps the perfect illustration of the proverb, "Man proposes, but God disposes." That is, whatever a man may plan for himself, the way he finally will walk is in the hands of God. St. Paul had planned to visit Rome as a free man—to stride boldly into the Eternal City with the Eternal Gospel. He first wanted to deliver the offering of money he had collected from the Gentile Christians abroad to the poor Jewish Christians of Jerusalem. Then, when that was accomplished, he would travel to Rome and preach the Gospel there, using Rome as his base for journeys even further afield—even as far away as Spain (see Rom. 15:22–29).

It was, however, not to be. Whatever the apostle proposed, God had something else in mind. When he came to Jerusalem, he was mobbed in the Temple by unsympathetic Jews, who assumed that he had brought the Gentile Trophimus within the Temple's sacred confines (Acts 21:27–30). Paul was arrested by the Romans for starting a riot and was kept in confinement. When he learned of his adversaries' schemes to assassinate him on the way to trial in Jerusalem, he used his Roman citizenship to appeal to Caesar, to be tried by his emperor in Rome (Acts 25:1–12).

So it was that St. Paul arrived in Rome under arrest and shackled to a Roman guard, awaiting his trial there. Even so, however, he had a measure of freedom. For a full two years he remained under house arrest, with freedom in his own rented quarters to welcome those who came to him from all over, preaching the Gospel to them with unhindered boldness (Acts 28:30, 31).

And many indeed came to him, bringing news of his churches and of the challenges they faced. He received news of heresy spreading in the Lycus Valley, threatening the work in Ephesus and its surrounding area, and in Colossae. The situation with his young friend Onesimus, a runaway slave Paul had converted while in prison, needed resolving also.

To address these issues, St. Paul wrote his epistles to the church at Colossae; to his friend Philemon, who had a house church there; and to the churches of Ephesus and the surrounding Asia Minor. After writing to the Colossian church, it would seem that St. Paul wanted to send a general message of teaching and encouragement to the communities surrounding Ephesus—communities which he had never actually visited, but which had been formed through his wider influence.

This was in the spring of AD 61. Delivery of the letters was entrusted to his friend Tychicus, who, accompanied by Onesimus (a runaway slave who had formerly belonged to Philemon), carried these letters to Asia Minor. He delivered the Ephesian epistle first to Ephesus and then took it as a circular letter to the surrounding churches of Asia. He also delivered the epistles intended for the Colossians and for Philemon.

Meanwhile, Epaphroditus, a presbyter of the church in Philippi, arrived in Rome with the Philippians' gift and support for St. Paul. St. Paul sent him back to his church in Philippi with an epistle thanking them for their gift, commending Epaphroditus for his service, and encouraging the church there. In the following spring of 62, Paul's trial before Caesar finally came up. To the delight of his churches (and the chagrin of his foes), he was acquitted and released.

So it was that the great Apostle to the Gentiles continued writing his epistles even while in prison. He may have been fettered and shackled to a series of Roman guards, but the Word he preached remained unfettered and free.

This volume contains commentaries on the epistles that St. Paul wrote while in prison. For ease of reference, the commentaries on his Epistles to the Philippians, Ephesians, Colossians, and Philemon are all self-contained, so that they may be consulted individually.

Key to the Format of This Work:
• The translated text is first presented in boldface type. Italics within these biblical text sections represent words required by English syntax that are not actually present in the Greek. Each translated text section is set within a shaded grey box.

> 12 **Now I intend you to know, brothers, that the things concerning me have come even more for the advancement of the Gospel,**
> 13 **so that my bonds in Christ have become manifest in the whole Praetorian *Guard* and to all the rest,**
> 14 **and that most of the brothers, becoming confident in *the* Lord because of my bonds, are more abundantly daring to speak the Word fearlessly.**

• In the commentary sections, citations from the portion of text being commented upon are given in boldface type.

He would have them know that his circumstances actually **have come even more for the advancement of the Gospel.**

• In the commentary sections, citations from other locations in Scripture are given in quotation marks with a reference; any reference not including a book name refers to the book under discussion.

As the apostle said elsewhere, "It is no longer I who live, but Christ who lives in me" (Gal. 2:20).

• In the commentary sections, italics are used in the ordinary way—for emphasis, foreign words, etc.

The word translated here *advancement* (Gr. *prokope*) is a military term.

❧ The Epistle of St. Paul the Apostle to the Philippians ❧

St. Paul in Philippi

The city of Philippi was a little bit of Rome in the midst of Macedonia. It had been founded by (and named for) Philip, the father of Alexander the Great, and in the days of Caesar Augustus it became a Roman colony. Like all Roman colonies, it modeled itself after Rome and prided itself on its Roman connection. Its citizens spoke the language of Rome, dressed like Romans, used Roman titles for their magistrates, and kept their loyalty to Rome front and center in their civic lives. There was a border garrison of Roman soldiers stationed at Philippi, as the city was on the main road from Rome to Asia. When St. Paul came to plant the cross in Philippi, he was, in principle, declaring his intention to convert and transfigure the whole Roman world.

The apostle was led to Macedonia by the special work of the Holy Spirit. In approximately AD 52, he and his apostolic companions were passing through the region of Galatia. Proceeding west, they attempted to journey into Asia and then north into Bithynia, but were persuaded not to do so by the prophetic utterances of the Christians there. Instead, they continued further west to the port city of Troas (Acts 16:8). While in Troas, St. Paul had a vision in the night—a man of Macedonia appeared to him, saying, "Come over to Macedonia and help us!" St. Paul concluded that this was why the prophetic Spirit had forbidden his sojourn into Asia and then Bithynia. He was instead meant, by divine Providence, to head further west into Macedonia, planting the first church on European soil (Acts 16:9, 10).

As was his usual custom, St. Paul went first to his Jewish compatriots. The Jewish community in Philippi must have been quite small, for it appears they did not possess a building of their own. Rather, they had a place of prayer by the riverside, which seems to have been frequented mainly by Jewish women and Gentile God-fearers (that is, Gentiles who worshipped the Jewish God but without actually taking the step of becoming Jews). St. Paul and his companions went there to join them in prayer on the Sabbath.

Of the women to whom they spoke, one from the city of Thyatira, named Lydia, paid special attention to the apostolic message. She had a business selling the purple goods for which Thyatira was famous. As purple fabric was very costly, Lydia must have been quite well off. At length she took the step of accepting the Christian message and, with her household, received Holy Baptism from the apostle. St. Paul and his group then accepted hospitality at her house, making it their base of operations while in Philippi (Acts 16:12–15). Through patient work, a number of people were converted and added to the church.

One day, while the apostles were on their way to the Jewish place of prayer by the riverside, they met a slave girl who was used by her owners for fortune-telling. The poor Asiatic girl was tormented and used by a "Pythonic spirit" (Gr. *pneuma Pythona*). That is, she was possessed by a spirit supposedly given by Apollo, the god associated with the giving of oracles, who was worshipped at the Pythian shrine at Delphi. Her demented utterances were taken for oracles, and this brought much gain to her owners, who shamelessly exploited the poor girl. She followed the apostles everywhere they went, shrieking, interrupting, and calling out that they were servants of the Most High God.

After a long time the apostles had had enough and turned to the girl, saying to the demon, "I charge you in the Name of Jesus Christ to come out of her!" The spirit immediately left her and the girl returned to normal, dazed but free. The girl's owners, however, knew that their hope of making money from her was gone, and in retaliation they dragged the apostolic leaders, Paul and Silas, before the secular authorities to lodge a complaint. Fueling the owners' rage was not only the fact that the apostles had (as they thought) damaged their "property" (i.e. the slave girl). Also significant was the fact that the apostles were Jews—not ethnic Romans, or even Greeks like most of Macedonia. They were members of the despised Jewish race, trying to foist their inane Jewish superstitions on the Gentile world—"customs which it is not proper for us Romans to accept" (Acts 16:21). An anti-Semitic mob rose up against the apostles, and the magistrates had them stripped, severely beaten with rods, and thrown into the common jail with their feet in the stocks. Luke and Timothy (who were Gentile and half-Gentile, respectively) remained with Lydia and the rest of the believers, praying for their companions.

Their wounds still bleeding and their backs in great pain, Saints Paul and Silas nevertheless lifted up their voices in prison, singing the hymns of the Psalter and praising God for the privilege of suffering for Him. All the other prisoners heard this and were amazed. Other men spent the night cursing their captors—these men spent the night blessing God! What kind of men were these?

About midnight, a great earthquake shook the prison. All the doors were thrown open and all the stocks jarred loose. The jailer, pledged to guard the prisoners with his life, saw the open doors and thought that all had escaped. In a terrified agony of mind, he planned to kill himself with his short sword, for death was the only penalty for one who let his prisoners escape. Then the voice of St. Paul rang out in the darkness: "Don't hurt yourself—we're all here!" (Such was the awe in which the prisoners held these two strange men that they had allowed the apostles to persuade them to stay where they were.) The jailer (a Roman citizen from the sturdy middle class) called for lights. He ran to where they were, saw them safely there, and knew he could stand no more. He gave in to the stirrings which had gripped his heart as he listened to the apostles' singing. Falling down, he asked, "How can I be saved like you?" The apostles' message of faith in Jesus Christ was received by his penitent and trembling heart and he was baptized that very night, along with all his family in their home nearby.

The magistrates considered that the punishment of the previous night was enough for the troublemaking Jews and they sent to release them, only to receive a shock themselves: Paul and Silas were

Roman citizens. It was a gross violation of their rights to have bound and beaten them without proper trial. At St. Paul's insistence, the magistrates came and apologized publicly, courteously requesting the apostles to leave. Since it was time for the apostolic band to move on, they visited Lydia and the fledgling church one last time before departing for Thessalonica (Acts 16:16–40).

Despite their being in Philippi for such a short period of time, the bonds of love which were forged between St. Paul and his little flock were deep and lasting. They sent offerings of money to help support the apostle several times: after he had just left them to travel to Thessalonica, they sent a gift not once but several times (Phil. 4:16); and after he had left Thessalonica and arrived (at length) in Corinth, they sent another gift to him, hearing that he was in need (2 Cor. 11:9). That St. Paul accepted these gifts is significant and indicates an especially close bond between him and the Philippians, for he made it a well-known policy and point of pride that he did not accept gifts from anyone (2 Cor. 11:9–12). That he made an exception in their case showed the deep love between them.

While St. Paul was imprisoned in Rome, in perhaps the fall of 62, Epaphroditus, a presbyter from Paul's beloved Philippian church, arrived with yet another gift for him. Epaphroditus, however, was in bad shape: the rigors of the trip to Rome had left him seriously ill, so much so that he almost died. Upon his recovery, St. Paul resolved to send him back, even though he desired to stay with St. Paul and serve him there. St. Paul hoped to send Timothy to the Philippians as a go-between at some later time, but for now Epaphroditus was to return to Philippi. And return he did, bearing the epistle of St. Paul for them.

❦ The Epistle to the Philippians ❧

§I   Opening Greetings (1:1, 2)

❧ ❧ ❧ ❧ ❧

1 1   Paul and Timothy, slaves of Christ Jesus, to all
the saints in Christ Jesus who are in Philippi,
with the bishops and deacons:
2   Grace to you and peace from God our Father
and the Lord Jesus Christ.

St. Paul omits his usual self-designation and description "called
to be an apostle" (see Rom. 1:1) and here simply styles himself the
slave of Christ Jesus. It is unusual for St. Paul to omit this assertion
of his apostolic dignity. His usual custom is to place his apostolic
authority at the head of his epistles, to give weight to what he is
going to say. With his beloved Philippians, however, he knows that
this is unnecessary, for they will love and obey him without this
formal assertion of his apostolic authority. Thus he is content to
refer to himself simply as the **slave of Christ Jesus**. That is, he serves
the Lord with unconditional obedience, even as a slave serves his
master. He shares this apostolic servitude with **Timothy**, with whom
he associates himself as the author of the letter, even though, as is
apparent, the contents of the letter come solely from himself. He
does this because St. Timothy is with him, visiting him in his imprisonment, and because the Philippians know Timothy, since he
was with St. Paul in the original evangelization of Philippi.

St. Paul then makes reference to the local clergy, the **bishops
and deacons**. This singling out of the local clergy is unique in Paul's
epistles, which elsewhere simply refer to the local church as a whole.
No doubt he makes a point of addressing them here because of his

gratitude for the gift the Philippians have sent him (delivered by the hand of Epaphroditus), since these clergy were instrumental in the organization of that gift.

A word may be said about the term *bishop* (Gr. *episkopos*) as used in the first century. The bishops of the local churches then were the local leaders and shepherds of each community. The term properly means "overseers." It is used in the NT interchangeably with the term *presbyters*. (Compare Acts 20:17–38, where St. Paul calls to himself the "presbyters" of the Ephesian church [v. 17] and addresses them as "bishops" [v. 28].) In the first century, the local church in each city was ruled by a plurality of leaders. Each of these leaders oversaw his own little house-church subsection of the local community and was styled its "overseer" or bishop. Taking a verbal cue from Judaism with its local "elders" (Gr. *presbyteros*), these leaders were also called "elders" or presbyters.

One of the leader-bishops in each city was also the coordinating bishop, with the function of representing the entire local church. In Jerusalem, the coordinating elder-bishop was James (see Acts 12:17; 15:13; Gal. 2:12). It was not, however, until the early second century that a special title was selected for this office. Up until this time, the terms *presbyter* and *bishop* were used interchangeably for the offices of *all* the leaders. By the second century, the term *bishop* was reserved for the office of coordinating leader alone, while the term *presbyter* remained to designate the rest of the leaders. The second century therefore did not see the creation of the office of the single "monarchical" bishop. This function of "monarchically" coordinating all the others remained from the apostolic days of the first century. What was new in the second century was the creation/limitation of the title *bishop* to designate this office.

St. Paul then opens with his usual apostolic greeting of **grace . . . and peace.** "Grace to you" (Gr. *charis umin*) was the usual Greek secular greeting and meant no more than wishing someone joy and happiness. In the work of St. Paul, however, it becomes more than simply a form of greeting. It is a solemn and prayerful invocation of God's grace and favor. Similarly, the common Jewish greeting of "Peace" (Heb. *shalom*) originally meant no more than "hello." But in the mouth of St. Paul, it is a bestowal of the peace and Presence of Christ.

As in his other epistles, St. Paul associates the Lord Jesus with God the Father as the Giver of **grace** and **peace**. This witnesses to St. Paul's belief in the full deity of the Lord Jesus, since He is one with God as the Giver of grace and life.

§II   Opening Thanksgiving—for support in his imprisonment (1:3–8)

ॐ ॐ ॐ ॐ ॐ

3   I thank my God in my every remembrance of you,

4   always in my every supplication for you all making supplication with joy,

5   in view of your sharing in *the preaching of* the Gospel from the first day until now,

6   being persuaded of this very thing, that He who began a good work in you will perform it until the day of Christ Jesus.

7   For it is only righteous for me to think this *way* on behalf of you all, for I have you in my heart, since both in my bonds and in the defense and confirmation of the Gospel, you all are co-sharers of grace with me.

8   For God is my witness, how I long for you all with the heartfelt *love* of Christ Jesus.

Letters in ancient times customarily began with thanksgiving. St. Paul begins his letter here with thanksgiving for the faith of the Philippians. Whenever he remembers them before God in prayer, in every **supplication** for them, he gives thanks to God for their faith. Indeed, he makes his intercessory supplication **with joy**. Here we have one of the keynotes of this epistle—the joy of the Lord, which abounds even in circumstances of suffering, distress, and imprisonment. Paul may be in prison, but he is still filled with joy!

This joy comes, he says, when he thinks of them **in view of your sharing** [Gr. *koinonia*] **in** *the preaching of* **the Gospel . . . until now**. He remembers when they first accepted the Gospel and shared in it. The thought here is not primarily of their mere acceptance of the Gospel and of their own salvation. Rather, the thought is of their role in sharing the apostolic preaching of the Gospel *with others* by their continued prayerful and financial support of St. Paul. Time and again, they have shared with him in his task of preaching, helping to make his ministry possible—which holy work continues, he says, even **until now**. This is evidence of their loyalty to Christ. They are full of zeal, and it is this continuing zeal which comforts the apostle even in prison, filling him with joy every time he remembers them to God in prayer.

This zeal **persuaded** him that God, **who began a good work** in them, would **perform it until the day of Christ**. The words translated *began* (Gr. *enarxomai*) and *perform* (Gr. *epiteleo*) are the technical terms used to describe the beginning of a sacrificial ritual and its completion. His description of God's work in their lives breathes this atmosphere of sacrifice. By using such language, St. Paul indicates that our lives are meant to be a living sacrifice to the Lord (see Rom. 12:1). In offering ourselves to the Lord, however, we are not left to rely solely on our own strength. Rather, God Himself aids us, for He is at work within our hearts "both to will and to work for His good-pleasure" (2:13). Between now and the final **day of Christ Jesus**, there will be many temptations and trials, much persecution to undergo, and many battles to fight. Nonetheless (as the Church sings at Great Compline), "God is with us!" He began this **good work** of making us a living sacrifice, and He will not abandon us until His work is done. The Philippians can therefore face the future fearlessly, with joy and confidence, knowing that God will be with them in their trials to complete His work in them. St. Paul has full confidence, he says, in their final salvation.

This is not mere flattery, the apostle insists. Rather, **it is only righteous for** him **to think this** *way*. His confidence in them is fully justified, he says, for they are one with him in all his trials and rewards. Though far away from St. Paul in his imprisonment in Rome, the Philippians still suffer for him and with him, anguishing over him and praying for him. There is an inseparable bond linking them to their apostolic founder. For his part, St. Paul **has** them in his **heart**, cherishing this bond and praying for them in return. Being one with him in spirit, they are **co-sharers of grace** (Gr. *sugkoinonos*) with him. That is, just as they suffer with St. Paul over his **bonds** and imprisonment and anguish over his upcoming trial and **defense . . . of the Gospel**, so they will receive the same grace and comfort from God that he does. For God has promised His special grace and Presence to those who suffer for Him (see Matt. 10:18–20; 1 Pet. 4:14). Even as the Philippians identify with their beloved apostle in his sufferings, so will they receive the same comfort and **grace** that he receives. Note the double use of the word *sharing* (Gr. *koinonia*) in verses 5 and 7: the Philippians share with St. Paul in helping him preach the Gospel (giving him money), and in return they are sharers with him of divine grace. It is this closeness with him and this experience of growth in grace that give St. Paul such confidence in their final perseverance until **the day of Christ.**

St. Paul's closeness to them is such that he cannot fully put it into words. Only **God** can **witness** and know how much he **longs for** them **all**. Indeed, he longs for them **with the heartfelt** *love* [Gr. *splagchna*] **of Christ.** The word rendered here as **heartfelt** *love* is difficult to translate. Literally, it means "intestines, heart, liver, lungs"—the "innards." It was used metaphorically to indicate the seat of the emotions. Any feeling which came throbbing straight from the heart, red-hot, was said to come from the *splagchna*. St. Paul here says that he loves the Philippians not with any ordinary affection, not with any merely human emotion, but with all the boundless, overflowing, heartrending compassion of the Lord Himself. It is, in fact, not that *Paul* loves them, but that the Lord Himself loves them *through* Paul. Our love is meant to be the conduit for the Lord's love and our lives the expression of *His* life. As the apostle said elsewhere, "It is no longer I who live, but Christ who lives in me" (Gal. 2:20).

§III   Opening Prayer—for their growth despite his imprisonment (1:9–11)

ॐ   ॐ   ॐ   ॐ   ॐ

9 And I pray this, that your love may abound yet more and more in real-knowledge and all discernment,

10 that you may prove the things that are excellent, in order to be sincere and unoffending to *the* Day of Christ;

11 having been filled with *the* fruit of righteousness through Jesus Christ, to *the* glory and praise of God.

As with all letters in those days, St. Paul's letter also opens with a prayer for his correspondents. He prays that their **love**, already much in evidence through their many gifts to him and their suffering with him in his imprisonment, may continue to **abound yet more and more**. The word translated here *abound* (Gr. *perisseuo*) indicates a great, overflowing, reckless bounty (see its use in Eph. 1:8 for the grace of God).

St. Paul does not, however, simply pray that their love may abound and become more plentiful. (Given the generosity of the Philippians, it does not appear that shortage of love is likely to be a problem for them!) Rather, he prays that their love may abound **in real-knowledge and all discernment**. The word here translated **real-knowledge** is the Greek word *epignosis*—not just "knowledge" (Gr. *gnosis*) but *epignosis*—a real, deep, and intimate knowledge. It is paired here with **discernment**, meaning keen moral discernment. St. Paul in fact doesn't want them to live and love indiscriminately. Their love must grow, but it must mature as well. Without this maturity, they might well be deceived by spiritual counterfeits, abundant in those days, who claimed to teach the way of love, while in fact walking in sin and error. It was too easy for the immature to confuse license with freedom!

St. Paul urges them to this maturity so that they **may prove the things that are excellent**. This "proving" is the process of recognizing true moral excellence and distinguishing it from spiritual laxity and decadence. Only by steering clear of these counterfeits (which offered religion without righteousness, in a kind of antinomian "situation ethics") can they hope to be found blameless on the Day of Judgment. Their task here and now is to discern what is truly pleasing to God and to perform it. They are to be **sincere and unoffending**—that is, pure and simple of heart (Gr. *eilikrines*— "unmixed, pure"), giving no cause for offense or scandal, persevering in this even **to** *the* **Day of Christ**. If they will exercise this moral discernment in their love, they will be **filled with** *the* **fruit of righteousness** and this will redound **to** *the* **glory and praise of God** on the Last Day.

St. Paul's prayer for the Philippians provides an antidote for the deadly modern notion of "religion as niceness." The only virtue enthusiastically applauded by secular society today is "tolerance," and any form of moral and ethical discernment, any condemnation of a behavior as sinful and wrong, is itself condemned as "not nice" and as "intolerant." The Lord's teaching has been reduced to the maxim (misunderstood by the world), "Judge not." In opposition to this counterfeit version of Christianity, St. Paul warns that true love *must* be critically discerning, able both to approve and embrace the morally excellent, and also to denounce and reject the morally objectionable. Only so can we hope to stand before the Lord our Judge at the dread and glorious Second Coming and endure the full sunlight and scrutiny of His gaze.

§IV   Good News from Prison—a reason for rejoicing (1:12–26)

> ঔ৽ ঔ৽ ঔ৽ ঔ৽ ঔ৽
>
> 12 Now I intend you to know, brothers, that the things concerning me have come even more for the advancement of the Gospel,

13 so that my bonds in Christ have become manifest in the whole Praetorian *Guard* and to all
the rest,

14 and that most of the brothers, becoming confident in *the* Lord because of my bonds, are
more abundantly daring to speak the Word
fearlessly.

15 Some, indeed, are heralding Christ even from
envy and strife, but some also from goodwill;

16 the latter do it out of love, knowing that I am
laid *here* for the defense of the Gospel;

17 the former proclaim Christ out of opportunism, not purely, supposing to raise up tribulation *for me in* my bonds.

18 What then? Only that in every way, whether
in pretense or in truth, Christ is announced;
and in this I rejoice. Yes, and I will rejoice,

St. Paul turns now to the main body and message of his epistle.
He begins with a note of comfort and assurance, telling the
Philippians not to mourn for him. His imprisonment is not something bad—rather, it is something good! It is a reason to rejoice! He
would have them know that his circumstances actually **have come
even more for the advancement of the Gospel.** The word translated here *advancement* (Gr. *prokope*) is a military term, denoting
the advance of an army as it cut its way through forest and moun-
tain. St. Paul uses the term here to show that his imprisonment does
not mean a setback for the Gospel. Rather, the Church militant,
like an ever-victorious army, continues its advance unimpeded.

How can this be? For one thing, the fact that his imprisonment
is **in Christ** has become known to the **whole Praetorian *Guard*.**
The Praetorian Guard were the elite, imperial guards, a select group
of nine cohorts of one thousand soldiers each, who functioned as a
kind of bodyguard for the emperor. They were stationed and garri-
soned in Rome. As St. Paul remained under house arrest, he would
have been chained to a soldier from this guard at all times, with the

attending soldier rotating every day or so. St. Paul, of course, used this as an opportunity to preach the Gospel to the soldier, who was a kind of captive audience. As the months went on and the guards were rotated, St. Paul eventually had the opportunity to speak to very many of this Praetorian regiment, and, as the soldiers gossiped among themselves, sharing news of this strange Jewish preacher they had been guarding, news of the Gospel spread throughout **the whole Praetorian *Guard*.**

This was important, because St. Paul's detractors were only too happy to suggest that he was in prison for treason or some other criminal activity. But as the soldiers from the Praetorian Guard soon discovered, he was not under arrest for any really criminal activity at all, but simply for the cause of Christ. This news eventually spread to **all the rest** in Rome who heard about Paul. What was the final result? That **most of the brothers** in Rome, who were formerly fearful of declaring themselves to be members of the possibly treasonous sect of Christians, now had **become confident in *the* Lord** and were **more abundantly daring to speak the Word fearlessly.** The widespread attention received by Paul and his Christian message— that his religion was *not* treasonous, but good and loyal—helped them as well. Now they too were heartened to share their Faith with others, since St. Paul's case had prepared the way for them.

Some of those speaking **the Word** of the Gospel were, to be sure, no friends of St. Paul. The Christians in Rome were a mixed bag. Some were supporters of St. Paul: they identified with him as a valiant apostle and brother in the Lord, sympathizing with him since his imprisonment was **for the defense of the Gospel.** They **heralded** the Gospel (Gr. *kerusso*—cognate with *kerux*, "a herald") out of **love** and **goodwill** for Paul, hoping that their further spreading of the Gospel would encourage him.

Some in Rome were *not* supporters of St. Paul. This is hard for us today to imagine, since we are so used to reading about him as *Saint* Paul, the great Apostle to the Gentiles, "the herald of the Faith and teacher of the universe" (from the *apostikha* for the Feast of Ss. Peter and Paul, June 29). But in those early days, his true stature and worth were not immediately apparent to all. Some Christians in Rome (especially the Jewish Christians there) may not have liked him at all. They may have thought him to be needlessly provocative and a troublemaker. Serves him right to end up in prison!

These seem to have wanted to take the opportunity of Paul being out of the way to further their *own* ministries and popularity at his expense. They proclaimed the same Gospel as he did, but did so from impure motives. They were motivated by **envy and strife** and worked out of **opportunism** (Gr. *eritheia*). The word translated *opportunism* meant originally simply "working for pay," but came to imply being a hireling and having selfish political ambition. Its use here indicates that some Christians in Rome considered Paul to be a rival. They envied him his success and fame and wanted to detract from him whenever they could. In this way, they thought that Paul would find his detainment in prison **bonds** even more frustrating and galling and a source of even more **tribulation** and distress.

What then? St. Paul asks. If his rivals and detractors think that he will be distressed at their progress, they are much mistaken. He has a far nobler heart than they do, and he cares only for the progress of the Gospel, not for his own popularity. For whether Christ is proclaimed **in pretense or in truth**—whether through pure motives or selfish, still **Christ is announced**! In this fact, St. Paul rejoices.

He takes care to stress this rejoicing to his Philippian hearers, for he began the epistle with this good news in order to comfort them. He wants to show them that his bonds are not a bad thing and should not be a source of grief to them. Rather, they are a good thing. Much good has come out of them. Because of his imprisonment, the Christians in Rome are proclaiming Christ with greater boldness, and this is a real reason to rejoice! All has happened, in the Providence of God, for the greater **advancement of the Gospel**.

ॐ ॐ ॐ ॐ ॐ

19 for I know that this will turn out for salvation for me through your supplications and *the* provision of the Spirit of Jesus Christ,

20 according to my earnest-expectation and hope, that I will be ashamed in nothing, but that with all boldness, as always, *so* even now Christ will be magnified in my body, whether by life or by death.

21 For to me, to live *is* Christ and to die *is* gain.

22 If *it is* to live in *the* flesh, this *will mean* fruit of work for me; and I do not know what I will choose.

23 But I am impelled from two *sides*, having the desire to be released and be with Christ, for that is very much better;

24 yet to remain-on *in* the flesh is more necessary for you.

25 Persuaded of this, I know that I will remain and remain alongside you all for your advancement and joy of the faith,

26 so that your boasting may abound in Christ Jesus in my *case* through my coming to you again.

In verse 18, St. Paul was determined to rejoice, saying, "Yes, and I will rejoice!" (These words belong to the verses that follow [1:19f], not to the preceding verses [1:9–18a], for v. 19 begins with the preposition **for**, connecting it to the immediately preceding "Yes, and I will rejoice" of v. 18b.)

The apostle's determination to rejoice in the future is based on his expectation that his entire prison experience will ultimately result in his release (**salvation**, Gr. *soteria*) and thus will finally have accomplished nothing but good. He here uses the word *salvation* in its original Hebraic sense of "rescue, deliverance." (Compare Ps. 69:1, where the Psalmist prays for Yahweh to "save" him, meaning to deliver him from the attacks of his foes.) It is in this historical, noneschatological sense that the Church in her litany prays for "captives and their salvation."

This ultimate release will be accomplished **through your**

supplications and *the* **provision of the Spirit of Jesus Christ**. Note
the synergy that characterizes all of God's work with the children of
men. He is the Savior, the Rescuer, the Deliverer, but we have our
part to do as well. He provides the Spirit, but we must make our
supplications. His grace and help work side-by-side with our own
willing efforts, so that the divine grace perfects created nature. God
will not override or dishonor the human will, for it is the crown of
His creation.

It is apparent from these verses that St. Paul does not want only
to be released, but also to have the opportunity to speak. He wishes
the imprisonment to result not just in his acquittal, but in his triumphant witnessing to Christ before Caesar (see Eph. 6:19, 20). In
this as in all things, St. Paul thinks first not of himself and his fate,
but of the Gospel.

Thus, he wants the Philippians to offer **supplications** for him
to stand firm and proclaim Christ boldly at this trial. This will be
possible through the **provision** and support of **the Spirit of Jesus
Christ**, given by God in answer to the **supplications** of the
Philippians. That is, through their intercessions, the Spirit will give
to St. Paul everything he requires. (The word translated here *provision* is the Gr. *epigoregia*, meaning literally "to pay for a choir"—a
fairly costly expense in those days! Its use here by St. Paul shows
how abundantly and lavishly God provides for us.) It is as the Lord
said: in the fateful hour of public martyric witness, the Spirit will
teach His disciples what they are to say (Matt. 10:19, 20). St. Paul's
only desire is that, when that hour comes, he **will be ashamed in
nothing**—that he will not deny Christ or compromise the Gospel
before Caesar, the intimidating master of the world. Rather, St. Paul
wants to proclaim the Gospel **with all boldness**, holding nothing
back, so that **Christ will be magnified in** his **body**. That has always
been his only desire: that in all things, with every breath, in any and
every circumstance, **whether by life or by death**, Christ's greatness
might be proclaimed by him. His trial before the great Caesar is his
great opportunity to magnify the Lord Christ, and he prays that he
will be equal to the opportunity.

This is what is important to him. His life is of comparative

EPISTLE TO THE PHILIPPIANS

insignificance. Even if he were to die (as one day he must), if the trial were to result in his execution—so what? **To live** means only communion with Christ (see Gal. 2:20). **To die**, then, would mean even closer communion with Christ, so that his death would be his **gain**! How can he lose? What does it matter whether he lives or dies? If he is acquitted and **lives in *the* flesh** after his trial, the result will be the **fruit of work**. That is, he will continue his glorious apostolic work for his Lord. And if he is *not* acquitted, but executed, he will then **be released** from this life **and be with Christ**, united in even closer communion with Him than now—and **that is very much better**. He confesses himself, when he thinks of purely personal considerations, to be **impelled from two *sides***. He could be happy with either one, with either acquittal and life or execution and death. He wants to be with his Lord in heaven. He wants also to stay with his beloved churches, for that is **more necessary for** them. Thus, he tells them, the outcome of his trial is not to be feared either way.

After talking about his possible death at such length, St. Paul returns to comfort his Philippians, almost as if the possibility of his death would be too unsettling and traumatic for them. He adds quickly, **Persuaded of this, I know that I will remain and remain alongside you all**. Certainly, he has written to comfort them and does not want to alarm them now! So he adds his assurance that he will indeed surely be released, even though he has been talking about the possibility of his death. Convinced that his continued life of **fruit of work** among them is **more necessary for** them, he **knows** that he will not die, but remain alongside them. So he comforts them, like a father comforting his children (see our Lord comforting His disciples in John 16:6, 7). He will not only **remain** (Gr. *meno*) alive, he will also **remain alongside** them (Gr. *sumparameno*; the second verb is built on the first)—for what is in their heart is not merely that Paul should not die, but that he should stay with them, visiting them, comforting them, caring for them. It is his remaining with them that is their desire! It is this of which St. Paul assures them.

The Philippians have cause to boast in Christ for their steadfastness in the faith. The apostle comforts them by promising them that through his acquittal and **coming to** them **again**, they will have further reason to **boast in Christ** as they glorify and exalt Him as the One who has answered their prayers.

§V   **Exhortation to Unity—a comfort to St. Paul while in prison (1:27—2:18)**

ॐ ॐ ॐ ॐ ॐ

27 Only conduct yourselves *as citizens* worthy of the Gospel of Christ, so that whether having come and seen you or *being* absent, I may hear about you that you are standing *firm,* in one spirit, *and* one soul, co-competing for the Faith of the Gospel;

28 not intimidated in any way by opponents— which is a demonstration of destruction for them, but of salvation for you, and that too, from God.

29 For to you it has been given for Christ's sake, not only to have faith in Him, but also to suffer on behalf of Him,

30 having the same contest which you saw in me, and now hear *to be* in me.

St. Paul begins his exhortation to unity with the word **only**— this is the only thing he asks of them, as a comfort to him while in prison: that they live worthy of the Gospel, keeping a serene unity, even in the face of mortal danger. This is an indication of how important St. Paul considers unity to be, for in all his concerns for them, this is the **only** thing he asks. Whether he can **come and see** them soon or remains incarcerated, he wants to hear of their stability and unity.

This stability and unity are manifest when they **conduct** themselves *as citizens* (Gr. *politeuo*) in a manner worthy of the Gospel. This word is cognate with the word for "citizenship" (Gr. *politeuma*).

St. Paul in fact here exhorts them to live as citizens of the Kingdom. Philippi was a Roman colony, and its Roman citizens took great care to conduct themselves as befitted Romans, cherishing their Roman citizenship. In the same way, St. Paul exhorts them to cherish their Kingdom citizenship, living worthily of their true King.

Thus, what St. Paul wants for his Philippian converts is this— that they **stand** *firm* (Gr. *steko*). The word means not just "to stand," but "to stand still, to wait steadfastly." In the face of any **opponents** and persecution, they are to remain unflinching. And not just unflinching, but united—in **one spirit** (Gr. *pneuma*) and **one soul** (Gr. *psuche*), **co-competing for the Faith**. Persecution and fear tend to divide, as each one looks out only for himself and flees away from the others (see the Apostles' flight from the Lord in Gethsemane, Mark 14:50). St. Paul's desire is for them to remain united in motivation (**spirit**) and in purpose (**soul**—see Acts 4:32, where the Jerusalem church was of "one heart and one soul" in their purpose of supporting the poor among them). They are not to back down in fear, startled and unnerved, each man deserting his post and abandoning the others. They are to share the same desire to keep the Faith, the same purpose of confessing Christ, even in the face of suffering.

He desires that they remain united in this way as they **co-compete for the Faith**. The word **co-compete** (Gr. *sunathleo*) savors of the Games, for the verb *athlete* means "to compete in the arena." As Christians, they too are called to competition, though not for earthly rewards or an earthly victor's crown (see 1 Cor. 9:24, 25). They are to compete together, as a united family of spiritual athletes, in the arena of Faith, for the imperishable crown of eternal glory. Like God's gladiators, they are to fight the good fight together.

In this struggle, they are **not intimidated in any way by opponents**. The word **intimidated** (Gr. *pturo*) is not the usual word for "fear," but a much stronger word, meaning "to be terrified," startled into running away. (It is the word used for frightened horses.) This is no doubt what their persecutors expect—that they will collapse in fear, being intimidated and cowed. St. Paul exhorts them to **stand** *firm* as they strive together for the Faith and not to be at all alarmed or **intimidated** by threats and bullying. This will be a clear **demonstration** and proof that God is with them. Their opponents can clearly see by the Christians' fearless serenity that they themselves are doomed to **destruction** if they persist, while the Christians are destined for **salvation**. This **demonstration** (the Philippians' fearless serenity) is **from God**—that is, it is God's sign and communication to the unbelieving society to surrender and not to fight against His Church. It is His message and warning to the world, telling them of the divine origin of the Gospel. In saying this, St. Paul encourages the Philippians to be fearless and steadfast. This is how important your courage is, he tells them—it is the sign God gives to the world, to call them back to repentance!

And this persecution which they will undergo, he tells them, is not a calamity from the world; it is a gift from God! You have been **given** by God (Gr. *charizomai*, cognate with the word *charis*, "grace"), granted as a gracious gift, not only to **have faith** in Christ, but also to **suffer** for His sake. They have recognized God's grace and goodness in their believing Him. They must see His goodness to them in this experience also. Their suffering is a great gift from Him, for it is through this that they will win their victor's crown of imperishable glory (see Rom. 8:17).

The Philippians are now involved in the same spiritual arena as St. Paul. With him, they share the same **contest** (Gr. *agona*). The word for **contest** once again savors of the gladiatorial games or athletic competitions. (In Heb. 12:1, it is used for the "race" of faith.) They **saw** him involved in this contest themselves, when he was beaten and thrown in the Philippian jail (Acts 16:22–24). They now **hear** about his struggle in the Roman prison. It is this same **contest** that they themselves now experience. Thus St. Paul encourages them. For they feel one with St. Paul and long to be with him and to share his suffering. The persecution you experience, he tells them here, is one way you *can* be with me, sharing my experience. You in Philippi and I in Rome—we are united in the same bond, sharing the same **contest** of suffering for Christ.

ॐ ॐ ॐ ॐ ॐ

༄ ༄ ༄ ༄ ༄

2 1 Therefore if there is any encouragement in Christ, if there is any consolation of love, if there is any sharing of *the* Spirit, if any heartfelt *love* and compassions,

2 fulfill my joy by minding the same *thing*, having the same love, joined-in-soul, minding the one *thing*.

3 *Do* nothing from opportunism or empty-glory, but with lowly-mindedness esteem one another as of greater importance than yourselves;

4 do not look out for your own *things*, but also for the *things* of others.

Having showed them how important is their unity in the face of persecution, St. Paul goes on to implore them to have this unity among themselves. If there is anything at all to be gained by their Christian experience together, let them keep this unity! If they get anything back at all—any **encouragement** and aid (Gr. *paraklesis*) from their experience of Christ, any **consolation** that comes from loving one another; if they have any experience of sharing and fellowship through the Spirit's power (Gr. *koinonia*), if there be any **heartfelt** *love* or inner yearning for one another (Gr. *splagchna*) or **compassions**—he implores them—then keep this precious unity. Then he will be filled with **joy**, even in his imprisonment.

He thus implores them to **mind the same** *thing* and keep the same attitude of humility before each other. He asks them to have **the same love**, with everyone concerned to meet his neighbor's need. He exhorts them to be **joined-in-soul** (Gr. *sumpsuchos*), having a common purpose—that of seeking the common good. He repeats again that they must **mind the one** *thing*, as of supreme importance—they must have as their one and common goal the preservation of unity. None of their actions should be motivated by base **opportunism** (Gr. *eritheia*; see 1:17) or wanting to appear as better than the other. This would be mere **empty-glory**, vain illusion and useless conceit. Rather, they should esteem their neighbor and his needs as of greater importance than themselves, in true **lowly-mindedness**. This **lowly-mindedness** is not a morbid or pathological lack of self-esteem. Rather, it is the healthy determination to serve one's neighbors before oneself and to make their needs a higher priority than one's own. It refers to the unassuming modesty of the servant, who finds joy in giving—of the one who **looks out** for opportunities to serve. If they will cultivate these qualities among themselves, St. Paul says, his joy will be complete!

ॐ ॐ ॐ ॐ ॐ

5   Have this mind among you, which *was* also in Christ Jesus,

6   who, although He existed in *the* form of God, did not esteem that to be equal with God *was* a thing to be seized,

7   but emptied Himself, taking *the* form of a slave, and having become in *the* likeness of men

8   and being found in appearance as a man, humbled Himself, becoming obedient to death, even *the* death of a Cross.

9   Therefore also, God highly-exalted Him, and gave Him the Name which is above every name,

10 so that at the Name of Jesus every knee should bend, of those who are of the heavenlies and of the earthlies and of the subterraneans,

11 and that every tongue will confess that Jesus Christ *is* Lord, to *the* glory of God the Father.

St. Paul continues to encourage them to **have this mind** and attitude among themselves—the one which is given to them by the life and example of the Lord Jesus. He is the perfect example of a humble attitude, one that seeks the good of the other, no matter what the personal cost. He displayed this attitude for us through

His own Incarnation, so that our Christian ethics are rooted in Christology.

Some suggest that St. Paul quotes here from an already-existing hymn, celebrating the Incarnation of the Lord. If this is so, it is seamlessly incorporated into his epistle. (Also, scholars cannot agree about its supposed poetic form. Some say the hymn contains two strophes of three verses each, while others say it contains three strophes. Since so much subjectivity is involved in identifying it as a separate, self-contained hymn, the most likely conclusion is that it is *not* a separate hymn, but rather the work of St. Paul, composed on the spot as a part of this epistle.)

St. Paul gives us the Lord Jesus as an example of humility. In doing so, he focuses not just upon this or that earthly act of Christ (e.g. His Entry into Jerusalem on a donkey or His washing the disciples' feet). Rather, he focuses upon the Incarnation itself as an act of humility, and one that sets the stage for our Lord's entire life of humility. He describes both the descent of Christ and His subsequent ascent, both His "downward" self-abasement and His "upward" glorification. The Lord Himself embodies His word, "He who humbles himself will be exalted" (Luke 18:14).

In describing Christ's voluntary "descent," St. Paul first describes Him as having **existed** [Gr. *uparcho*] **in** *the* **form of God**. The word translated *existed* is a stronger verb than the verb "to be." It indicates a continued, nontentative, unchanging form of subsisting. Christ existed **in** *the* **form of God**—that is, stable and sovereign, having all the attributes and characteristics of Deity, being one with the Father. Nonetheless, He did not esteem that having His being in a manner **equal with God** was **a thing to be seized**. He did not clutch it like a precious treasure, refusing to let it go. On the contrary, He **emptied Himself** by **taking** *the* **form of a slave**. In His love for us, He willingly exchanged the position and privilege of the highest for the position and humiliation of the lowest. His **form** (or essential character and mode of existence, Gr. *morphe*) went from that of the Deity to that of the servant; from being adored by myriads of angels and archangels to being the Carpenter of Nazareth who had no place to lay His head. Without ceasing to be divine, He assumed humanity also for our sake. Through His Birth from the all-holy Theotokos, He became **in *the* likeness** [Gr. *omoioma*] **of men**, being found **in appearance** (Gr. *schema*) as a man. The terms translated *likeness* and *appearance* do not deny the reality of the Incarnation. They do *not* mean that He was simply "like" a man, that He only "appeared" to be human, but was not human in reality. Rather, they mean that Christ was *like* all men everywhere, no different from them at all, sharing their full human nature. His **appearance** (or outward manifestation, manner of being, deportment) was that of a human being. He lived in the world as a true Man among men, able now to look up as well as down.

In this state, He further **humbled** Himself, embracing lowliness and humility, obeying the divine will of the Father, even though it meant **death**. And not just any death, but the most ignoble, shameful and agonizing of deaths—*the* **death of a Cross**, a fate Rome reserved only for the most hated of its criminals. From the highest, Christ stepped down in humility, descending even to the lowest.

We see the result of such humility: exaltation and glory. It was because of Christ's humbling of Himself to the depths that **God highly-exalted Him** by giving Him the Name and rank above all others. Note that it is Christ's obedience *in His human nature* which is rewarded (see Heb. 5:7–10). For though His two natures, divine and human, are inseparable, it was still in His humanity that He suffered. And it was this divine-human Christ, "the Man Christ Jesus" (1 Tim. 2:5), who was rewarded with the gift of exaltation. For though He remained God during the days of His flesh and throughout His earthly life, as a human being He still partook of our lowly station. After He **humbled Himself** to *the* **death of a Cross**, this lowly state was His no more. As the reward for obedience, God bestowed upon Him an exalted place at His right hand.

Christ's exalted rank is now superior to that of all other beings—both angels and men, both the living and the dead. He rules over those angels and powers in **the heavenlies** (Gr. *epouranios*; see its use in Eph. 3:10). He rules over all those of **earthly** existence (Gr. *epigeios*), the children of men who live on the earth (Gr. *ge*). He rules even over those of **subterranean** existence (Gr. *katachthonios*), those departed spirits in Sheol, the land of the dead. All of creation must therefore **bend the knee** in homage **at the Name of Jesus.** His exaltation is absolute and universal. **Every tongue** must one day **confess** that **Jesus Christ** *is* **Lord.** This will redound to the final **glory of God the Father**, as God will then be all in all, the Father glorified in the glory of His Son (see John 17:1).

The word used for *Lord* (Gr. *Kyrios*) has a special meaning in this context. It means that Jesus, the humble Carpenter of Nazareth, will be acknowledged as the absolute Master of the cosmos, the undisputed King over all creation, His sovereignty serene and un-troubled, neither challenged nor questioned. The term *Kyrios* is thus a strong one, indicating absolute ownership. It was thus the word chosen by the Septuagint translators to translate the Divine Name "Yahweh" of the Hebrew Old Testament into Greek. In describing Jesus as *Kyrios*, St. Paul uses the strongest word possible in his day. To be sure, the word *kyrios* could be put to lesser uses (see its use describing earthly masters in Eph. 6:9). But its use in this context indicates the totality of divine authority and glory for Jesus, the Son of Man and Son of God.

Behold, St. Paul says to his beloved Philippians, the ultimate reward of humility! Christ gave us an example of the attitude that should characterize our lives also. Like Him, we should humble ourselves in looking out not only for our own interests but also for the interests of others. The reward of Christ's humility and obedi-ence to the Father is the promise of our reward also, if we obey as He did.

ༀ ༀ ༀ ༀ ༀ

12 Therefore, my beloved, as you have always obeyed, not as in my presence only, but now much more in my absence, accomplish your salvation with fear and trembling;

13 for it is God who is at work among you, both to will and to work for His good-pleasure.

Having set Christ before the Philippians as an example and incentive to humility, St. Paul goes on to encourage them to holiness and perseverance. In giving this encouragement, he speaks with the utmost tenderness and gentleness, as understanding the difficulties they must face. Thus he addresses them as his **beloved**. He calls them to **obey** him in this, but it is the obedience offered to a loving father.

What he asks of them is to **accomplish your salvation with fear and trembling**. They had done this before when he was present with them in Philippi, and now that he is absent and in prison, he asks the consolation that they strive **much more** to accomplish this. The word *to accomplish* (Gr. *katergazo*) means "to achieve, produce, create." It is used in Ephesians 6:13 in a military context, meaning there "to accomplish heroic feats." St. Paul here tells the Philippians to strive to fulfill their salvation, producing this mighty work. They should strive, not proudly, as if puffed up by their own efforts, but rather **with fear and trembling**—that is, in humility. (The phrase **with fear and trembling** does not denote a cringing servility, but simply a nonreliance upon their own strength. St. Paul used the phrase of himself and his work in Corinth when he said he was with them there in "much fear and trembling" [1 Cor. 2:3], resolving to know nothing but "Jesus Christ and Him crucified.")

The Philippians should strive with all their might to accomplish salvation, but they should do so in humility, **for it is God who is at work among you**. They are not striving on their own, left by God to struggle in the midst of a hostile world. God has not abandoned them, but is in their midst! It is He Himself who **works among** them. It is as St. Peter says: if the One they invoke as "Father" is among them, they should pass their time in fear (1 Pet. 1:17), not presuming on His Presence, but mindful of His judgment.

God **works** in their midst and in their hearts; His power is operative and effective. The Greek word used is *energeo*—a verb often used to indicate a supernatural working (see its use in Matt. 14:2). And what He effects is **to will and to work for His good-pleasure**, to fulfill His will. That is, God works to provide the **will** within us, healing our will and renewing our hearts in His new creation, so that instead of doing the things willed by the flesh (see Eph. 2:3), we are able to desire and love the Law of God (see Heb. 8:10). He also works to help us accomplish the **work** of righteousness itself, providing the power of His Spirit to actually do it (see Rom. 8:2). Thus, though we must ourselves **accomplish our salvation**, it is God who works among us, teaching, healing, and transforming us, so that it is all for His glory.

ॐ ॐ ॐ ॐ ॐ

14 Do all things without grumbling or questioning;

15 so that you may become faultless and innocent, children of God blameless in *the* midst of a crooked and perverse generation, among whom you shine as lights in *the* world,

16 holding fast *the* Word of Life, so that in *the* Day of Christ I may boast that I did not run in vain nor toil in vain.

17 But if I am indeed poured-out-as-a-drink-offering upon the sacrifice and offering of your faith, I rejoice and co-rejoice with you all.

18 In the same way, you too rejoice and co-rejoice with me.

St. Paul continues to exhort his readers to peace, calling them to strive for holiness in the midst of the unholy and turbulent world around them. **Do all things without grumbling or questioning**, he says. The word translated here *grumbling* (Gr. *goggusmos*) is a word with a history. It is an onomatopoetic word, the syllables reproducing a low, grumbling, murmuring sound. It is the word used in Numbers 16:41 (LXX) for the open rebellion of the children of Israel against the leadership of Moses and Aaron. In response to this "grumbling," this threatening murmur of seething and armed insurrection, "they were destroyed by the Destroyer" (1 Cor. 10:10), as God sent a sudden plague which wiped out more than fourteen thousand of them (Num. 16:49). Thus, what St. Paul here forbids is not the usual petty complaining under our breath that often escapes our lips in our thoughtlessness (though this is not good either). What is forbidden is the rebellious questioning of God's goodness. When disasters and persecutions overtake us, it is tempting to rebel against God and say that if He really loved us, this would not happen to us (see Prov. 19:3). Such **grumbling** is deadly and to be avoided. It is paired here with **questioning**. Again, the **questioning** that is banned is arguing with God, disputing with Him as did Job, denying His providential goodness and care.

Thus, instead of hardening their hearts in adversity, they are to show themselves **faultless and innocent**. Their loving meekness in the face of persecution and suffering will set them off from the **crooked and perverse** world around them. The world will see that there is no cause to fault them for any crime and that they are **innocent** of anything that could merit their persecution. (The word for *innocent*, Gr. *akeraios*, is the same word used when our Lord told His disciples to be "wise as serpents and innocent as doves" in Matt. 10:16.) Thus, as the **blameless children of God**, they will **shine as lights in *the* world**. Their blameless holiness is not for themselves alone. Rather, it is a sign and **light** to the world, shining like the sun and moon (Gr. *phoster*; see Gen. 1:14 LXX), dispelling the darkness and showing them the way home to safety and salvation (Matt. 5:14). Seeing their example, the world need no longer walk in darkness.

They are not only to **do all things without grumbling or questioning**; they are also to **hold fast *the* Word of Life**. That is, they are not to surrender or lose their grip on the Gospel, nor to apostatize under pressure of persecution. Thus, if they will finally reach salvation on the Last Day of Christ, St. Paul says he may **boast that** he **did not run in vain nor toil in vain**. The athletic race of his apostolic ministry will not have been for nothing, if only they will hold fast to the Faith. Here is a mighty incentive for the Philippians to persevere—for if they do not, their beloved Paul will feel that he has toiled all for nothing!

In thinking about the Last Day, St. Paul considers the possibility of the trial ending with his execution and martyrdom. Even this possibility (though not expected—see 1:25) does not dampen his joy. All sacrifices in antiquity were accompanied by a libation or drink-offering poured out over the top of or alongside the sacrifice. St. Paul is responsible for the conversion of the Philippians, so that it is he who offers them and their faith to God as a **sacrifice and offering**. His death and shed blood would then be but the customary **drink-offering poured out** over the sacrifice. His martyrdom would but seal and complete his work in them—it would all be quite proper!

If this were to happen, he would **rejoice** (Gr. *chairo*) before God. More than that, he would **co-rejoice** (Gr. *sugchairo*) with them, inviting them to rejoice along with him in his martyrdom and glory. Here a great challenge is given to the Philippians. Certainly the death of their beloved apostle is something they dread and against which they pray. His death would leave them distraught and desolate. On the contrary, says St. Paul, my death would be a great joy to me! And you must share this joy, he says, not grieving, but rejoicing along with me! It is **the same** with their own sufferings, he goes on to say. They must **rejoice** in their own suffering for Christ and share their martyric joy with him. St. Paul does not consider persecution and martyrdom to be a calamity, but the bringer of eternal glory. Thus one should rejoice in them, and those who see such persecution should congratulate (one of the meanings of the Gr. *sugchairo*) the sufferer on his good fortune!

§VI   Future Planned Visits (2:19–30)

৯৵ ৯৵ ৯৵ ৯৵ ৯৵

19 But I hope in *the* Lord Jesus to send Timothy to you soon, so that I also may be heartened when I know the things concerning you.

20 For I have no one of kindred-soul who will genuinely be worried for your welfare.

> 21 **For they all seek after their own** *things*, **not those of Christ Jesus.**
> 22 **But proof of him you know, that like a child** *to* **his father,** *so* **he served** *as slave* **with me in the Gospel.**
> 23 **Therefore I hope to send him at once, whenever I see** *how* **things** *will go* **concerning me;**
> 24 **and I am persuaded in the Lord that I myself also will be coming soon.**

St. Paul now turns to his intended visit. He plans to send Timothy to Philippi, so that he can visit them and then return to St. Paul, bringing news of how they are. (He makes this plan **in** *the* **Lord**, that is, conditional upon it being God's will; see James 4:15.) This will **hearten** him (Gr. *eupsucho*, from the literal Greek for "to do well for the soul"), when he learns that they are steadfast in the Lord. See how St. Paul's own contentment and courage depend upon the welfare of others, since he loves them as being part of the same Body with him. In the same way, our hearts should be joined to others in our Christian communities.

In preparation for his own visit, he commends Timothy to them, saying that he is **of kindred-soul** with him (Gr. *isopsuchos*—literally, "equal-souled"). That is, Timothy is of the same purpose as St. Paul, for both of them are **genuinely worried** for the Philippians. The other Christians around St. Paul in prison (the local Roman Christians, we may assume—St. Mark and St. Luke being elsewhere) are not like him. They tend to put their own convenience and plans ahead of their service to **Christ Jesus**. But not Timothy—he seeks only the Lord's will and their welfare! The Philippians know of his proven worth themselves, for when both Paul and Timothy were in Philippi, they saw Timothy relating to Paul as a **child** to his spiritual **father, serving** *as slave* with him in the preaching of the Gospel (Gr. *douleuo*, cognate with the word for "slave," *doulos*). Thus they should welcome Timothy as they would welcome Paul. He will send him as soon as there is news for him to bring. And, taking thought as always to comfort them, he adds that he trusts **in the Lord** (which is to say, again subject to God's will) that he too will come to see them **soon**.

ॐ ॐ ॐ ॐ ॐ

25 But I esteemed it necessary to send Epaphroditus to you, my brother and co-worker and co-soldier, who is also your apostle and offerer to my need;

26 for he has been longing for you all and was homesick because you heard that he was ailing.

27 For indeed he was ailing coming near to death, but God had mercy on him, and not only on him but on me also, so that I would not have sorrow upon sorrow.

28 More eagerly therefore did I send him so that when you see him again you may rejoice and I may be less sorrowful about you.

29 Welcome him then in *the* Lord with all joy, and hold such *ones* in honor;

30 because he came near to death for the work of Christ, gambling with his life to fill up what was lacking in your offering to me.

Here St. Paul comes to one of the main purposes of his letter. He writes not only to comfort and encourage them, not only to thank them for their gift, but also to commend to them the bearer of the letter, their own Epaphroditus. No doubt they intended him to stay longer with St. Paul, caring for him as their representative. And here he was, back again, leaving St. Paul still alone in prison! Many in Philippi would want to reproach Epaphroditus with forsaking his sworn duty and running out in the middle of a job. So it is that St. Paul takes care to send him back with a commendation for his service, so that he will not suffer reproach upon his return home. It is entirely characteristic of St. Paul that, in prison and on trial for his life, he still selflessly takes thought for such lesser matters as the embarrassment and feelings of a brother.

St. Paul begins his commendation by explaining that it is *his* decision to send Epaphroditus back home, in saying **I esteemed it necessary**. It is not the case that Epaphroditus wanted to leave and St. Paul acquiesced. The decision originated with St. Paul, so that if there is blame attached to the decision, the blame is his, not Epaphroditus's. He goes on to commend him with a series of titles, describing him as his **brother, co-worker**, and **co-soldier**. In this, he seeks to identify Epaphroditus with his own apostolic work and rank, praising him as if he were an apostolic colleague, not just a convert and courier from one of the local churches.

As well, he goes on to describe him as **your apostle** (Gr. *apostolos*) and **offerer** [Gr. *leitourgos*] **to my need**. Neither of these two lavish praises translates well into English. **Apostle** of course means simply "messenger, ambassador," and this is all that Epaphroditus really is. He is a messenger from Philippi, bringing a gift and offering to stay and care for St. Paul. But in calling him **your apostle**, St. Paul means to further identify him as his beloved colleague. It is as if he is saying, "I am your apostle—and so is your own Epaphroditus, my colleague in the apostolic work!"

Finally, St. Paul describes him as **your offerer to my need**. The word translated *offerer* (Gr. *leitourgos*, or "liturgist") was used in the Greek Old Testament to describe priestly ministry (see Num. 18:2 LXX). An **offerer** was the one who offered the sacrifices. St. Paul describes Epaphroditus as their **offerer** because, to meet his **need**, Epaphroditus gave him their gifts of money, described further as "an acceptable sacrifice" to God (4:18). The Philippians' gift was accepted by God as a sacrifice—one offered, says St. Paul, by their **offerer** and sacrificing priest, Epaphroditus. In using this imagery, St. Paul would have the Philippians show Epaphroditus the same respect that the children of Israel owed to their priests.

St. Paul further says that the reason he is sending Epaphroditus home is that the latter fell ill and almost died. Whether because of the rigors of the journey or some other reason, the Philippian messenger was **ailing coming near to death**, and this at length became known to the church back home. He has been distressed at what they must be worrying (what with family and friends wondering if he would die or was perhaps already dead). Now that he has finally recovered, St. Paul **more eagerly** sends him back home, so that, upon learning he is well, the Philippians will **rejoice** and St. Paul himself will have one less worry about his beloved church there. In saying that he sends him so that the Philippians may **rejoice**, he subtly undercuts any temptation they may have to reproach him for deserting his post. St. Paul expects them to **rejoice** when he returns, not mourn and complain!

Finally, he explicitly tells them to **welcome him . . . with all joy, and hold such** *ones* **in honor**. His sickness and brush with death was not the result of carelessness, but was **for the work of Christ**. Not only that, he even heroically **gambled with his life** (Gr. *parabouleuomai*)—a gambler's word meaning "to risk everything on the roll of the dice." He took these risks in order to **fill up what was lacking in your offering** [Gr. *leitourgia*] **to me**. In other words, St. Paul says, there is nothing lacking in Epaphroditus! It was to make good *your* lack (i.e. your inability to deliver the offering because of distance) that he took such dreadful risks. Surely he should be greeted with a hero's welcome—not with reproach!

§VII   Warnings Against False Teachers (3:1—4:1)

ॐ ॐ ॐ ॐ ॐ

3 1   **For the rest, my brothers, rejoice in** *the* **Lord. To write the same things again** *is* **not troublesome to me, and it** *is* **a certainty for you.**

2   **Watch out** *for* **the dogs, watch out** *for* **the wicked workers, watch out** *for* **the mutilation!**

3   **—for we** *ourselves* **are the circumcision, who worship in** *the* **Spirit of God and boast in Christ Jesus and have no confidence in** *the* **flesh,**

4   **though I** *myself* **also might have confidence in** *the* **flesh. If another thinks to have confidence**

> in *the* flesh, I *myself have* far more:
> 5 circumcised the eighth day, of the race of Is-
>   rael, of *the* tribe of Benjamin, a Hebrew of
>   Hebrews; according to *the* Law, a Pharisee;
> 6 as to zeal, a persecutor of the Church; as to *the*
>   righteousness in *the* Law having become
>   faultless.

All **the rest** that he has to say in summing up is, **rejoice in *the* Lord**. With these words, St. Paul begins to close his epistle. It appears that he intends to exhort them to stand firm, to be united, to have peace (see 4:1–4). His concluding note is to be **Rejoice!** for the joy of the Lord is to be their source of strength in the persecution sweeping over them (see Neh. 8:10: "The joy of Yahweh is your strength"). Joy is the signature of the Christian. As Fr. Alexander Schmemann once said, "The most terrible of all accusations against the Christians was that they had no joy." The Philippians were to abound in joy, for joy is not a feeling, it is obedience to a command. Whether we are feeling euphoric or not, Jesus is still Lord, and it is that unchangeable fact in which we are to rejoice.

It would appear, however, that as St. Paul is thus concluding his letter, he thinks of their danger from the Judaizers. The Philippians are to **rejoice in *the* Lord** and **boast in Christ Jesus**, and this perhaps makes St. Paul think of the Judaizers, who rejoice and boast in the Law.

The Judaizers were a group of false Christians of Jewish background. They vehemently opposed Paul, denouncing him as a heretic and a perverter of the Faith. In their view, one could not be saved unless one was a Jew. Simple baptism and trust in the Lord's forgiving love were not enough; one had to be circumcised as well and keep the Law. Otherwise, one would be rejected by the Lord as an apostate unbeliever on the Last Day. St. Paul recognized this as a failure to understand the Gospel and as a perversion of the apostolic Faith. Nonetheless, the Judaizers were very zealous, and they followed St. Paul wherever he went, preaching and persuading, trying to undo his work, pushing circumcision on the new Gentile converts. Their teaching was rife throughout Galatia, where St. Paul had worked immediately before coming to Philippi (Acts 16:6–12).

With a vehemence of spirit born of worry for the Philippians, St. Paul denounces these Judaizers. He has warned the Philippians of these men before, when he was with them. But to **write** it **again** is no trouble at all, and the reminder will act as a **certainty** for them.

They are to **watch out** for the Judaizers—this warning is repeated for emphasis three times—and beware of these **dogs, wicked workers**, mutilators. To describe them as **dogs** means that they are contemptible, bold, and dangerous, for the dogs of that culture were not the pet dogs of today. They were wild dogs that roamed in packs, snapping and attacking whatever they could (see Ps. 59:14, 15). The Judaizers are likened to these dangerous, impudent, roaming packs. The Jews styled the Gentiles as dogs, but St. Paul says that it is the Judaizers who are the true dogs.

Also, they are **wicked workers**. They claim to be promoters of good works, righteous upholders of the commandments. St. Paul knows that their **work** or fruit is **wicked**. They do not work good, but rather wickedness through their perverting of the pure Gospel. Finally, they are described as **the mutilation** (Gr. *katatome*)—a play on words. The **circumcision** of which they boast is in Greek *peritome*. St. Paul says that *they*, the non-Judaizers, are the *true* circumcision— these Judaizers do not represent the authentic circumcision at all. *Their* circumcision is a mere **mutilation**—not a *peritome* but a *katatome*. It has no spiritual value, but only serves to mutilate and disqualify for true spiritual worship. For to refuse to trust Christ's love and to rely on something else in addition (such as circumcision) is to "fall from grace" and to be "severed from Christ" (Gal. 5:4).

St. Paul then talks about the central issue raised by the Judaizers: the place of merit and self-deserving in the Christian Faith. St. Paul says that he is representative of the *true* **circumcision**, the authentic Faith of Israel. This faith **worships in *the* Spirit**, not in the flesh. Their access to God is by the Holy Spirit (see Eph. 2:18), not by sacrifices in the Temple. Their **boast** and reliance is on **Christ Jesus** and His compassion and love, not on being circumcised. Their

confidence is not **in *the* flesh**—that is, in their earthly and physical pedigree. The Judaizers trust that being Jewish will save them, and they work to amass an impressive resume to present to the Lord on the Last Day. St. Paul knows that we need and can trust only in His mercy.

But his refusal to trust in his Jewish pedigree is not because he doesn't have one! If they want a pedigree, he can show them a pedigree! He was **circumcised the eighth day** as the Law required, **of the race of Israel** (not a Gentile proselyte), of the aristocratic **tribe of Benjamin** (the tribe that gave Israel its first king, Saul, and that remained loyal to David), a true and pure **Hebrew** (not a Hellenistic Jew), and a **Pharisee** (a member of the sect with the strictest interpretation of the Law). And if one wants to talk about zeal for the ancestral Jewish faith—well, he was **a persecutor of the Church** (see Gal. 1:13, 14)! One couldn't get a more impeccable Jewish pedigree than that! As to all the demands of the Law, he has **become faultless.** No Jew can point to any rigorous discipline that he has omitted. If personal merit and self-deserving give one **righteousness** and good standing with God, he certainly has that! But as a matter of fact, personal merit has no place at all in securing the favor and pardon of God.

ॐ ॐ ॐ ॐ ॐ

7   But what things were gain to me, those things I have esteemed as loss for the sake of Christ.

8   But even more, I esteem all things to be loss because of the surpassing importance of knowing Christ Jesus my Lord, for whom I *have experienced* the loss of all things, and esteem *them* crap so that I may gain Christ,

9   and be found in Him, not having a righteousness of my own from Law, but that which is through faith *in* Christ, the righteousness which comes from God *based* on faith,

10 that I may know Him and the power of His

---

resurrection and *know* a share of His sufferings, being conformed to His death;

11 if somehow I may attain to the resurrection from the dead.

12 Not that I have already received it or have already become perfect, but I pursue *it* that I may lay-hold of that for which I also was laid-hold of by Christ Jesus.

13 Brothers, I *myself* do not reckon myself as having laid-hold of *it*; but *I do* one thing: forgetting the things behind and stretching out to the things before *me*,

14 I pursue *the* goal for the prize of the upward call of God in Christ Jesus.

15 Therefore, as many as *are* perfect, let us have this mind; and if in anything you have a different mind, God will reveal that also to you;

16 however, let us keep walking-straight by that same rule to which we have attained.

His Jewish pedigree could have been treasured by St. Paul as **gain** and as something to wave before the face of God at His Judgment. Certainly, this is the way of his ancestral Pharisaic Judaism and the way that is assumed by the Judaizers. If one is to be saved, they feel, one needs to amass merit, to assemble a self-defense. But to truly **know Christ Jesus** is to know the embracing love of God. The experience of grace in Christ convinces Paul that salvation consists not in self-assertion and defense, but in humbly receiving forgiveness and pardon. Through Christ, penitent sinners, devoid of excuse, are welcomed home. Prostitutes and tax collectors need simply repent and be sorry for their sins in order to receive salvation and peace (see Matt. 9:10; Luke 7:36f). Here there is no place for self-defense, for pleading our merits or for offering excuses. Faced with our sins, we have come to know that there *are* no excuses and no real defense. Nor are any needed. God's grace in Christ embraces us as we are, making our little **righteousness** irrelevant. To draw back from this overwhelming embrace of love in order to preserve our pride and make our defense is to spurn the love of God and reject His pardon.

Thus St. Paul says that his supposed **gain** of Jewish pedigree and defense he esteems as **loss** and harm to himself, for if he brought it into account to make use of it, it would come between him and the pardon of God, the true and saving knowledge of **Christ Jesus my Lord**.

It is not only that he is prepared to throw away reliance on his Jewish pedigree. **But even more** (a difficult series of Greek particles to translate; an approximate rendering would be "Yes indeed, and then some"), he is prepared to part with **all things** and count them as loss as well in order to know Christ. Nothing can compare with knowing Christ—not family, wealth, security, or popularity. He has already *experienced* **the loss** of all these things in his apostolic ministry to Christ. He does not mind losing them if this is what it takes to know the Lord and finally **gain Christ**.

What does he care for all that life can give? If it comes to a choice between these things and gaining Christ, he will throw them away as if they were just so much **crap**. (The word *crap* is a good English word, found in the Oxford Dictionary and corresponding exactly to the Greek word *skubala* used here—a word meaning both rubbish and excrement.) He will part with the whole wide world as a worthless thing, if only he can gain Christ on the Last Day! He wants only to **be found in Him** . . . **having** . . . **the righteousness which comes from God** *based* **on faith**. That is, he does not want to have to rely on his own little **righteousness from Law**, depending upon a list of good deeds, fulfilled commandments, and amassed *mitsvoth*. Given the extent and enormity of his sins (see Rom. 7:18), that would be a woefully inadequate defense!

Rather, he wants his **righteousness** and good standing with God to be based on the divine forgiveness, the free gift given on the basis of his discipleship and **faith** *in* **Christ**. Only then can he hope to **gain Christ** and eternal life. For God does not want our carefully drawn-up list of accomplishments; He wants our heart. This is the ultimate issue in all discussion of the place of merit and self-deserving in the Christian Faith: What does God want from us? The Judaizers think that He wants an impressive score; that it matters not how proud our hearts are before Him, so long as we have accumulated a store of good deeds and avoided the blame He seems so ready to give. Inwardly, they think Him to be "a hard man" (see Matt. 25:24), quick to condemn, a dangerous God against whom we can protect ourselves if only we keep the Law rigorously enough. St. Paul knows better. He knows that what God really wants is *us*: our love, the response of our penitent and broken hearts. He knows that God is not quick to blame, but is a gracious and good God, and the Lover of mankind.

St. Paul thus says that he counts all things as loss in order to **know** Christ **and the power of His resurrection**. He refers here to his present experience. Even now, having given up all things to be His apostle, he knows and experiences **the power of His resurrection** and shares in **His sufferings**. As an apostle, he lives a life of suffering, hardship, and persecution (see 2 Cor. 6:4–10; 11:23–27) and it is through this **share** (Gr. *koinonia*) in the sufferings of Christ that he is **conformed to His death** and that the Cross of Christ, in all its power, is manifest in his life.

For as the Cross is manifest in his life, so too is **the power of His resurrection**. Life, strength, healing, and joy flow into his life as he suffers for his Lord. As he has said elsewhere, he is "constantly being delivered over to death for Jesus' sake that the life of Jesus also may be manifested" in his mortal flesh (2 Cor. 4:11). It is through this present experience of suffering for Christ that he hopes that he may **somehow attain to the resurrection from the dead**. The path to resurrection glory is, for him as apostle, through this formidable suffering—of which his imprisonment in Rome is a part. No matter: Let any suffering come, so long as he attains this final goal!

So now is not the time to rest. He confesses that he has not yet **received** the final **prize** (v. 14) of eternal life. He has not yet **become perfect** (Gr. *teleioo*). The word *perfect* (Gr. *teleios*) does not here mean "sinless." Rather, it means to achieve full maturity, to reach the final goal. (Our Lord described His reaching His final goal on the third day as being "perfected," Luke 13:32; and the spirits of righteous men in heaven were described as being "made perfect," Heb. 12:23.) Thus St. Paul here says he has not yet reached the final goal or the maturity of the age to come.

Here he speaks with an eye on the Judaizers, for it appears that part of their appeal and sales pitch is that they offer spiritual maturity to the Gentiles. "Baptism is an acceptable beginning," they seem to have argued, "but to *really* reach spiritual maturity, you Gentiles need to be circumcised!" St. Paul here seems to answer them, "I am a circumcised Jew and even *I* haven't yet reached the maturity you Judaizers claim to offer!" Maturity, St. Paul counter-argues, comes not from going back to Judaism or from clinging to and claiming the accomplishments of the past, but from **forgetting the things behind and stretching out to the things before** him. All their past Jewish pedigree should be left behind as an encumbrance in the race they are called to run. Jesus Christ has seized hold of them so that they can **pursue . . . the prize of the upward call of God**, or the heavenly glory to which God has called them in Christ Jesus.

The imagery used is that of the footrace. To win the race and gain the prize, the runner must not look back (e.g. to his Jewish past). Rather, he must **forget the things behind** and keep his eyes on the finish line. Christ **laid-hold** of him for just this purpose— that he in turn may **pursue** this prize in order to **lay-hold** of it. With all his might, he must **stretch out**, straining, going flat out for the finish line. In such a race to **lay-hold** of the prize, there is obviously no place for looking **behind** to one's Jewish heritage. Any runner knows that to look back in the race is to cast away hope of winning.

Having exhorted the Philippians to leave the past behind and not to listen to those who would try to con them with the false promise of maturity, St. Paul ironically says to them, "As many of you as *are* **perfect** (or claim to be so) should have this attitude of mine! You want to be **perfect** and mature? Then listen to my advice! If you don't yet see my point, but have **a different mind** or attitude, God will reveal the truth to you in time." His opinion is not just his own opinion—it is the truth of God, and St. Paul claims that God will vindicate his teaching in the hearts of the Philippians.

However, he adds, **keep walking-straight** (Gr. *stoicheo*, "to walk in a straight line"), following the **same rule** [Gr. *kanon*] **to which we have attained**. Whatever God will reveal to you in the future, St. Paul concludes, will be consistent with what He has already revealed through the apostolic preaching, the Rule of Faith. They must continue to **walk-straight** in that way and not swerve off into heresy.

The mention of further revelation from God leads St. Paul to add this final warning, for God would not **reveal** anything contrary to the apostolic standard to which they have already attained. (Some MSS omit the word *rule* from this sentence, but the sense of the warning remains the same, whether the apostolic standard is stated or merely assumed.)

༄ ༄ ༄ ༄ ༄

17 Become co-imitators of me, brothers, and watch those who walk according to the pattern you have in us.

18 For many walk, of whom I told you often, and now tell you even weeping, that they are enemies of the Cross of Christ,

19 whose end *is* destruction, whose god *is* the belly, and *whose* glory *is* in their shame, who mind earthly things.

20 For our citizenship exists in *the* heavens, from which also we wait for a Savior, the Lord Jesus Christ;

21 who will transform the body of our humiliation *into* conformity with the body of His glory, by the working of the power that He has even to submit all things to Himself.

4 1 Therefore, my beloved and longed-for brothers, my joy and crown, thus stand *firm* in *the* Lord, my beloved.

He concludes his long warning against the Judaizers by telling them to become **co-imitators** of him. That is, they should all together, preserving unity, follow his example and conform to the apostolic **pattern** (Gr. *tupos*, "type"). There must be no disunity, no breaking of ranks! Let them *all* together imitate him in this! This **pattern** that they are to imitate is the apostolic example and teaching (see Rom. 6:17, which speaks of our being delivered to the apostolic "*tupos* of teaching"). More specifically, he refers to the example of apostolic reliance upon Christ alone and of finding in baptism one's full salvation. The forgiveness Christ offers there does not need to be supplemented or completed by any circumcision.

Not all follow this apostolic **pattern**. The Judaizers, though claiming to be Christians, are in fact **enemies of the Cross of Christ**. Not of course that they denounce the Cross, but their insistence on circumcision makes the Cross irrelevant (see Gal. 2:21). More than that, they want to avoid anything that would invite persecution from their fellow-Jews, insisting on circumcision "in order not to be persecuted for the Cross of Christ" (Gal. 6:12). St. Paul warned the Philippians of them before while he was with them (see 3:1), and now warns them **weeping**. Here we see again the great heart of the apostle of God. He can be polemical, lashing out furiously against his foes, denouncing them in harsh language as dogs, wicked-workers, mutilators (3:2). Yet for all that, he still desires their salvation, and the thought of their eventual destruction is a grief to him. He who could wish himself even "accursed and separated from Christ" for the sake of his unbelieving Jewish compatriots (Rom. 9:3) grieved also for the heretical adversaries of Christ. Here is the example for our own polemics. We must denounce unfaithfulness and heresy, but no hatred for the heretics themselves must enter our heart. We must love them enough to **weep** over their heresy and loss of salvation.

St. Paul gives a terse threefold description of his foes, revealing the truth about them. Their true end and final destiny is **destruction** (Gr. *apoleia*; see its use in Matt. 7:13). They claim to serve God faithfully so that their **end** and goal is eternal life, but they are misled. The way they are on leads to damnation, so the Philippians should therefore not follow them. Also, their true **god** is their **belly** or desires. They claim to be ruled by the God of Israel, but by creating dissensions, they show that they are in fact ruled by their own desires (see Rom. 16:17, 18) and that they care more for this than for the saving unity of the Church. Finally, he says, their true **glory** is in their **shame**. St. Paul's glory is in the maturity and holiness of the churches he has founded (see 1 Thess. 2:20). What they consider to be their **glory** is getting Gentiles to accept circumcision—to the Gentiles' spiritual destruction—which will prove to be not to their **glory**, but to their **shame**.

In fact, the Judaizers' whole orientation is earthly—earthly racial descent, physical circumcision, material keeping of the Law. Though they claim to be more spiritual than St. Paul, their earthly concerns and issues reveal their true earthly **mind** or attitude. But, St. Paul says, the true Christian focus is not on **earthly things**, but on Christ in heaven. We are no longer citizens of the earth. Our **citizenship exists** [Gr. *uparcho*—"to exist unchanging"; see its use in 2:6] **in** *the* **heavens**, where Christ is, seated at the right hand of God (Col. 3:1). The Romans of Philippi were proud of their Roman citizenship; St. Paul here tells the Christian Philippians to be proud of their heavenly **citizenship**, deporting themselves at all times as citizens of the Kingdom (see 1:27). And as citizens, they are to keep their **mind** on heavenly things. They are not to be concerned with earthly issues like circumcision and the Law, but to **wait for a Savior** from heaven (see 1 Thess. 1:10), living in eager expectation. When He comes, He will entirely do away with such physical concerns as circumcision—and even with the entire body! The physical **body of our humiliation** will be **transformed** into a tangible resurrection body. It will then be conformed to **the body of His glory**. Now we suffer the **humiliation** of sickness, the passions, and death. Then we shall share the Lord's glory and be filled with His **power**—even that same invincible power which He has **to submit all things to Himself** on the Last Day.

Having described the Judaizers' true characteristics, St. Paul **therefore** urges the Philippians to **stand** *firm* (Gr. *steko*—see 1:27) against them. He shows that he is motivated by his love for them, for he says how he longs for them even across the miles. They are his **joy and crown** of victory on the Last Day. He twice refers to them as **beloved**. Thus he ends his warnings with love, for love alone gives one the right of exhortation.

§VIII   Final Personal Admonitions (4:2–9)

> ॐ ॐ ॐ ॐ ॐ
>
> 2   I exhort Euodia and I exhort Syntyche to be of the same mind in *the* Lord.
> 3   Yes, genuine yokefellow, I ask you also to support these women who have co-competed with me in *the preaching of* the Gospel, together with Clement also and the rest of my coworkers, whose names are in the Book of Life.

Epistles in those ancient days usually ended with personal words of greeting (see Rom. 16), and this is no exception. **Euodia** and **Syntyche** were evidently two prominent women (see v. 3, which speaks of **these women**, i.e. using feminine pronouns) who had a tendency to quarrel. The exhortation is a strong one, for he uses the word **exhort** once for each of them—i.e. *not* "I exhort Euodia and Syntyche" but rather, **I exhort Euodia and I exhort Syntyche**. Thus he does not take sides, but strongly puts both in their place, pleading with them to **be of the same mind** and attitude—namely, that of humility before each other (see 2:2).

In this task he asks his **genuine yokefellow** (Gr. *syzugos*) to support them in their struggle to live in peace. It is not that he is vexed with these women. On the contrary, he asks for support precisely because he esteems them so highly: they **co-competed** with St. Paul as his fellow-athletes (Gr. *sunathleo*, see its use in 1:27) as part of a team with Clement (possibly the later bishop of Rome who wrote the famous Epistle of Clement) and with many other **coworkers**. Their work as co-athletes with St. Paul in his Gospel preaching probably took the form of offering him the use of their homes for the meetings of the church. With the others, their names were inscribed in **the Book of Life.**

This **Book of Life** is a concept rooted in the OT: just as an earthly king had a register of favored people, so the heavenly King kept a book of His friends and favored ones (see Ex. 32:32; Dan. 12:1). As true and faithful believers, all their names were also inscribed in this Book of God's favorites.

Who was this **yokefellow** whom St. Paul involves in helping these women to live in peace? No one can know for sure, and even in the early Church there were many guesses. Some suggested (perhaps because of 2 Cor. 6:14, which speaks of being "unequally yoked") that this word had a marital flavor, and that it was a reference to St. Paul's wife! This was in fact the interpretation of Clement of Alexandria—despite St. Paul's own assertion that he was unmarried (see 1 Cor. 7:7). Some today suggest that the word *syzugos* was a proper name, but there is no other trace of this word so used.

Quite tentatively, I would suggest the following interpretation. I would suggest that the word does have, in this context, a marital flavor, but that it was a reference to the husband of one of the women involved. Perhaps this unnamed man was the husband of one of them and the brother of the other one. If he was also one of the bishops and leaders of the church (see 1:1), the conflict of the women becomes quite explicable—if not inevitable! Perhaps both women hosted gatherings of the church in Philippi, and their quarrel had its roots in this rivalry. One woman exalted herself as wife of one of the bishops and the other as his sister. This would also explain why it was not necessary to name the **yokefellow** involved—for who else would have the right (or the courage!) to intervene except one who was "yoked" and/or related to these women? (The envisioned scenario is not much changed if St. Paul means that the husband/brother is *his* **yokefellow** in the sense of helping him to govern the church and not the **yokefellow** in the sense of being married to one of the women.) We note that St. John Chrysostom also surmised that this **yokefellow** was married to one of the women.

ॐ ॐ ॐ ॐ ॐ

4 **Rejoice in** *the* **Lord always; again I will say, rejoice!**

5   Let your forbearance be known to all men. The
     Lord *draws* near!

6   Be worried in nothing, but in everything by
     prayer and supplication with thanksgiving let
     your requests be made known to God.

7   And the peace of God, which surpasses all
     mind, will guard your hearts and your thoughts
     in Christ Jesus.

8   For the rest, brothers, whatever is true, what-
     ever is venerable, whatever is righteous, what-
     ever is pure, whatever is lovely, whatever is of
     good repute, if there is any virtue and if any-
     thing praiseworthy, reckon these things.

9   What you have learned and received and heard
     and seen in me, practice these *things,* and the
     God of peace will be with you.

It would seem that St. Paul here finally returns to the conclusion he began in 3:1. Again, he would end on a note of joy, telling
them to **rejoice** in Christ **always**, whatever the outward circumstances. Indeed, so important is this rejoicing that he repeats it twice:
again I will say, rejoice! His letter to the Philippians could in fact
be characterized as "the epistle of joy," for over and over he refers to
the joy of the Lord (see 1:3, 18, 25; 2:2, 17, 18, 28, 29; 3:1; 4:1).
Though St. Paul may be fettered and chained in prison, his joy
remains unfettered and abounding. From the narrow confines of
his imprisonment, he seems to leap for joy in the Lord (see Luke
6:23), unable to contain his boundless and loving enthusiasm. Here
too his pastoral heart comforts his beloved Philippians. It is as if he
would tell them, "Don't be sad for me! Rejoice in the Lord! Let
nothing stop you from rejoicing in Him!"

Also, within this life of rejoicing, he urges them, **Let your forbearance be known to all men.** The meaning of the word translated
forbearance (Gr. *epieikes*) is difficult to convey fully. It means that
we should be always ready to yield, gentle, mild, reasonable. It is
not the mild blandness of the weak, but the joyful graciousness of

spirit that delights in peace. It is used in Wisdom 12:18 of the kind forbearance of God. When under persecution, we are always tempted to shout back, to return evil for evil. On the contrary, says St. Paul, we should let our **forbearance** shine forth among all and not allow ourselves to be provoked. We can afford to be gracious and not avenge ourselves, for **the Lord *draws* near!** We can leave all to the wrath of God (Rom. 12:18–21) and trust that all will be sorted out at the Second Coming.

For our part now, even in the midst of persecution, we are to **be worried in nothing** (Gr. *meden merimnate*; see its use for Martha in her distraction, Luke 10:41). We are simply to offer our **prayer and supplication with thanksgiving** to Him who best knows how much we can stand and what we truly need. Then we will not be distracted and at our wit's end, but rather **the peace of God** will **guard** our **hearts and thoughts.**

This peace **surpasses all mind** (Gr. *nous*), all comprehension. It is not subject to our limited human understanding. In the midst of turmoil and persecution, it seems impossible that we should maintain such serenity, such fearlessness, such untroubled peace! But it is possible, only because the unconquerable **peace of God** stands at the heart's door to keep out invading trouble. Having made our **prayer** to God and offered Him our requests and **supplication**, we can leave all in His hands, offering **thanksgiving** for His invincible care.

As St. Paul begins his conclusion, he sums up all his exhortation by addressing them as **brothers**. That is, he is not lecturing to his subordinates, but encouraging his beloved and equal brothers. And he tells them to keep their focus on all that is beautiful in life. **Whatever is true, whatever is venerable, whatever is righteous, whatever is pure, whatever is lovely, whatever is of good repute, if there is any virtue and if anything praiseworthy**, they are to **reckon** and consider **these things**. In time of persecution and betrayal, the easy thing is to focus on the failures and sins of men—on the brutality of life, on the unfairness and the pain. This is not the way home to the Kingdom. Rather, their focus should be on whatever is true, pure, pleasing, and worthy of respect.

It is not here a case of "positive thinking." Rather, it is striving to see life sacramentally as being crammed with the gifts of God and discerning God's glory in the world. This is part of the inheritance and example they received from St. Paul while he was with them. While in the Philippian jail, for example, he did not curse and complain. Rather, he sang hymns to God (Acts 16:25), setting his mind on the glory of the Lord. In the same way, they should **practice** and do the things they have seen in him. Whatever they have **learned** as disciples (Gr. *manthano*; see the Gr. *mathetes*, "disciple"), whatever they have **received** as apostolic Tradition (Gr. *paralambano*; see its use in 1 Cor. 11:23; 15:1), whatever they have **heard** from his instruction—this should be their guiding principle. For the apostle takes care to teach by example also, not just by verbal precept (see 2 Thess. 3:6–9). It is in this way that they will enjoy the blessing of **the God of peace** in their community. The fullness of the Divine Presence will only rest upon them as they follow the apostolic precepts.

§IX   Added Final Thanksgiving for Their Gift (4:10–22)

ॐ ॐ ॐ ॐ ॐ

10 But I rejoiced in *the* Lord greatly, that now at last you have made your thought for me to flourish again; indeed, you took thought before, but you had no opportunity.

11 Not that I speak from a lack, for I have learned in whatever *circumstances* I am to be content.

12 I know *how to* be lowly, and I also know *how to* abound; in everything and in all things I have been initiated into *the secret* of eating-to-the-full and hungering, both of abounding and of lacking.

13 *I have* strength for all things through Him who empowers me.

14 Yet you have done well to co-share with me in my tribulation.

15 You yourselves also know, Philippians, that at the beginning of the *preaching of the* Gospel, when I went out from Macedonia, not one church shared with me in the account of giving and receiving but only you yourselves;

16 for even in Thessalonica you sent once and twice for my needs.

17 Not that I seek the gift, but I seek for the fruit that increases to your account.

18 But I have received-in-full all things *you sent* and I abound; I am full, having welcomed from Epaphroditus the things from you, an odor of fragrance, an acceptable sacrifice, well-pleasing to God.

19 And my God will fulfill all your needs according to His riches in glory in Christ Jesus.

20 Now to our God and Father be the glory to ages of ages. Amen.

He concludes by thanking them again for their gift of money. Comparing their **thought** and concern for him to a plant, he says once again it has **flourished**. Not, he hastily adds, that they took no thought before, but that they had no opportunity to send the gift before now. Again, he takes care not to give the wrong impression. He is not complaining of want, **lack**, or destitution, suggesting that he was miserable until their gift arrived. On the contrary, he has learned to be content, whether he has an abundance or whether he suffers want, whether he **eats-to-the-full** (Gr. *chortazo*—see its use in Rev. 19:21 for birds of prey gorging on the flesh of the slain) or whether he **hungers**. He has **been initiated into** *the secret* (Gr. *mueo*, a word used for initiation into the mysteries) of contentment. The secret is this: he has **strength** for all things, through the power of Christ. As he relies upon Christ, Christ enables him to have peace **in everything and in all things**, every circumstance and in all ways. His contentment no longer depends upon outward conditions, but upon the Lord. This is the secret of his invincible peace.

In saying that he was not miserable before their gift arrived, he also does not want to give the impression that he does not appreciate it. Their **co-sharing** (Gr. *sugkoinoneo*) with him in his **tribulation** and affliction is a noble thing. It is beautiful, fit, **done well** (Gr. *kalos*).

This is the sort of people they are, for when he was first *preaching the* **Gospel** there, when he had scarcely left their province of **Macedonia**, they sent him a gift. Indeed, when he had not even left Macedonia, but was still there in nearby **Thessalonica**, they sent him help—and not only once, but **twice**. No one else helped him in that way, **sharing** their money—**only** the Philippians.

Here he hastily adds yet another clarification—**not that** he **seeks the gift** itself. He considers this to be so important not because he wants their money. What he really wants is their spiritual progress— **the fruit that increases to your account**. He concludes his thank-you for the gift by assuring them that he has indeed **received** it **in full** (Gr. *apecho*, a technical term for receipt of goods in full). For when he says, **I seek for the fruit that increases to your account**, they shouldn't think that he hasn't yet received it but is still looking for it! On the contrary, faithful **Epaphroditus** fulfilled his task, delivering what they sent. And a true and **acceptable sacrifice** it is, one that will bring the blessing of God to their lives. (For sacrifices were offered in the hope of receiving the divine blessing.) They have fulfilled his needs, and his God, in turn, will **fulfill all your needs**. And He will do this with His customary generosity and grace— **according to His riches in glory in Christ**. That is, all the heavenly riches and blessings of Christ will be showered upon them in return. No wonder St. Paul ends his thank-you with the praise of God: to Him be **glory to ages of ages**.

ॐ ॐ ॐ ॐ ॐ

21 Greet every saint in Christ Jesus. The brothers who are with me greet you.

22 All the saints greet you, especially those of Caesar's house.

The final few lines are in accordance with epistolary convention. In those days, one finished by passing on greetings. St. Paul sends his greeting to **every saint** and believer the Philippians may meet. All the brothers with him in Rome send their greetings, **especially those of Caesar's house** or the slaves and staff of the Imperial household—those who are with St. Paul on the front lines—including perhaps many who converted through the influence of St. Paul through the Praetorian Guards.

§X   Concluding Blessing (4:23)

ॐ ॐ ॐ ॐ ॐ

23 The grace of the Lord Jesus Christ be with your spirit.

As in all his epistles, St. Paul ends with a formal apostolic blessing, leaving his beloved Philippians by commending them to the Lord. From his prison captivity, the great apostle reaches out to them, praying that the **grace**, favor, and protection of the Lord may be with their inmost **spirit**. So St. Paul of unfettered joy ends his epistle to them, leaving them with this note of peace.

❧ The Epistle of St. Paul the Apostle to the Ephesians ❧

St. Paul in Ephesus

The Ephesus of St. Paul's day was a major cosmopolitan city in Asia Minor and the capital of the surrounding area. As a busy port city, it was a market for many goods and services and a thoroughfare between East and West. It was full of bustle, prosperity, and confidence. It was also full of idolatry. Its chief architectural boast was the great and far-famed temple of the goddess Artemis (or Diana), brilliant in beauty and counted one of the wonders of the world. It measured 425 feet by 220 feet, had 127 columns, each 60 feet high, and housed (as did all pagan temples) the idol-image of the deity. The worship of Artemis was the subject of intense local patriotism, pride, and enthusiasm.

It is difficult to say how the Faith first came to Ephesus and through what now-nameless disciples of Christ the first seeds were sown. Certainly Apollos came to Ephesus early on. He was a believer in the Lord Jesus, though he had only experienced the baptism of St. John the Forerunner. He preached the Lord Jesus boldly in the synagogues of Ephesus and, when he met Priscilla and her husband Aquila, was persuaded to remedy the defects and gaps in his faith by receiving Christian baptism (Acts 18:24–28).

Later, Apollos left Ephesus for Corinth and St. Paul arrived. This was (perhaps) in the fall of AD 54. There he found about a dozen of Apollos' old converts—disciples who believed in Christ, but who, like their teacher Apollos, knew only the baptism of John. St. Paul remedied the lack in their faith and experience, baptizing them with Christian baptism (Acts 19:1–7).

He then began the evangelization of Ephesus in earnest. As was his usual custom, he first entered the synagogue of his fellow Jews and preached the Gospel there. He was at first heard with interest, as a famous and controversial teacher in Israel. At length, though, his message was rejected. After about three months, as he continued to speak to them about Jesus as Messiah, their opposition grew and hardened into actual hostility. St. Paul knew that it was time to go. Taking with him those Jews from the synagogue who had accepted his message, he withdrew from the synagogue and began renting quarters in the Lecture Hall of Tyrannus (a place where a school of philosophy and rhetoric met) to teach the Faith there. Here he was to stay for two years, teaching, persuading, and disputing, so that not only those in Ephesus itself, but all the residents of the province of Asia heard of him. It was probable that the apostle worked at his trade of tentmaking during the morning and then offered classes in the afternoon, teaching the Faith to any who were interested (Acts 19:8–10).

This was a time of extraordinary fruitfulness for the Gospel in Ephesus and indeed in all Asia Minor. Church communities were founded in the towns and villages surrounding the great metropolis through the influence of St. Paul and his converts. He began to be quite famous, if not even notorious! God did many mighty miracles through His apostle, so much so that clothing that he had worn was taken away to be used as instruments of healing and exorcism—the first instance of "secondary" relics on record (Acts 19:11, 12). It was apparent that there was something special about Paul and his Christian message.

All knew of his success in casting out demons. A few itinerant Jewish exorcists, having heard of this success, thought that they too would capitalize on it. They attempted an exorcism "in the Name of Jesus whom Paul preaches." It was not a success. The demons responded, "Jesus I know and Paul I am acquainted with—but who are you?" and leaped upon them in violent retaliation, so that they were forced to flee, wounded and naked. When word got out about this, Paul was held in even higher esteem and many more joined the church. Some of these, renouncing their occult and pagan past, brought their books of magical arts to be publicly burnt. This spectacle also contributed to the high profile of the Gospel message (Acts 19:13–20).

At length, however, there arose public opposition to this growing Christian movement. It was probably in the spring of 57. Though St. Paul had not publicly attacked devotion to the goddess Artemis, everyone knew the Christian opposition to idols and that they said, "We ought not to think that the Deity is like gold or silver, a representation by the art and imagination of man" (Acts 17:29). It appears that sales of silver shrines of Artemis were down. One of the silversmiths, Demetrios by name, rallied his fellow-workers in opposition to Paul and his movement. The great festival of Artemis, held in May, was a time of projected sales, and they feared that if they did not take vigorous action now, they would be ruined.

Gathering his colleagues together, Demetrios denounced the Christians, appealing not only to the pagans' own economic self-interest, but also to their civic pride and religious fanaticism. "There is danger that this trade of ours may come into disrepute," he cried, "and also that the Temple of the great goddess Artemis may count for nothing. She may even be deposed from her magnificence!" The group quickly turned into a mob as they began chanting, "Great is Artemis of the Ephesians!" The whole city was in tumult and gathered at the huge public assembly building. All was in confusion as the chanting went on for about two hours. St. Paul, when he learned of this, wanted to go and address the crowd, but some of his friends wisely held him back. At length, cooler heads prevailed and the crowd broke up (Acts 19:23–41).

It was obviously time for St. Paul to leave Ephesus, and he did, after (we may imagine) bidding farewell to his friends and converts at the Hall of Tyrannus. He set sail for Macedonia and came, at length, to Corinth in the south by the wintertime (Acts 20:1, 2). From there he traveled north again to Macedonia.

That spring, he decided to return to Jerusalem, hurrying so as to be there for Pentecost. He traveled to Miletus, a few miles from Ephesus. From there, he called his old friends, the beloved presbyters of Ephesus, for one final meeting. They met with him one last time, weeping at the end, because they knew they would never see him again (Acts 20:38). He embraced them, kissed them, and boarded the ship for Jerusalem. It was in Jerusalem that he was indeed arrested and, through his own appeal to Caesar, at length brought to prison in Rome by the spring of AD 61.

The present Epistle to the Ephesians is part of St. Paul's prison legacy. It was written during a time of discouragement and difficulty when he was on trial for his life. Yet, despite all this, the epistle radiates a sense of almost ecstatic joy. The apostle is himself radiant and awestruck at the grace and kindness of God. Though himself chained and imprisoned in Rome, he never forgets that in Christ he is blessed beyond measure and sits with Him in the heavenlies. The Epistle to the Ephesians is the work of a man lost in admiration at the goodness of God in Christ.

❧ The Epistle to the Ephesians ❧

§I   Opening Greetings (1:1, 2)

❧ ❧ ❧ ❧ ❧

1   1   **Paul, an apostle of Christ Jesus through the will of God, to the saints who are faithful in Christ Jesus:**

     2   **Grace to you and peace from God our Father and the Lord Jesus Christ.**

The thought of his conversion on the road to Damascus **through the will of God** is never far from St. Paul's mind. He never forgot that he was formerly a persecutor of the Church (see Phil. 3:6) and that it was solely due to the mercy of God that he was now His apostle. This gratitude towards God was his incentive to "work harder than any of the others" (1 Cor. 15:10). Similarly, God's mercy to us should be our incentive to strive in serving the Lord.

Most manuscripts read, "To the saints who are *at Ephesus* and are faithful . . ."; only the Vatican and Sinaitic uncial manuscripts and the older Chester Beatty papyrus omit the Ephesian address. The present shorter reading, which sends the epistle **to the saints who are faithful**, omitting the words "at Ephesus," is almost certainly the authentic one. This epistle was meant as a circular, sent first to Ephesus as to the major city of Asia Minor, and then to the other smaller locations in the area.

The apostle sends his greeting of grace and peace **from God our Father and the Lord Jesus Christ.** Note the closeness of the two as the common giver of grace and peace. This witnesses to the full deity of the Lord Jesus. It is inconceivable that a Jew would consider a mere human being, however exalted, the associate of God, co-equally paired with Him in divine work—unless, that is, this Man were also true God. That Jewish St. Paul *does* pair the Lord Jesus with God the Father shows that St. Paul regarded the Lord as fully divine.

§II   Opening Thanksgiving—for God's salvation in Christ (1:3–14)

In this opening thanksgiving, St. Paul says that we should bless God, for His will for us is eternal blessing in Christ—our adoption as holy sons, which He accomplished in the Gospel—so that we should praise Him for His grace. In Christ we have full and rich redemption, which He lavishly poured out in all His grace. This redemption reveals God's hidden wisdom (revealed now through the Gospel) as a plan for the end times—viz. to unite all the cosmos with Jesus as Head. Thus we have become God's inheritance (according to the eternal plan of Him who makes everything in the world fulfill His purposes) so that we Jews might manifest His glory. In Christ, you Gentiles as well were claimed as God's own (by His giving you the Holy Spirit, the pledge of our final salvation, when God finishes His work)—so that you too might manifest His glory.

ॐ ॐ ॐ ॐ ॐ

3   Blessed *be* the God and Father of our Lord Jesus Christ, who has blessed us in Christ with every spiritual blessing in the heavenlies,

---

Like all letters of the ancient world, St. Paul's letters begin with an opening thanksgiving. Most of these epistolary thanksgivings begin with simply "I thank my God" (see Rom. 1:8), but here he explodes into a heartfelt benediction: **Blessed *be* God!** God (who is both **the God and Father** of the Incarnate Son) is blessed *by* us because He has first blessed us. Our doxology and love for Him are a response to His love for us.

Not only has God blessed us through our relationship with His

Christ, but He has blessed us **with every spiritual blessing**. That is, in Christ, we are given every blessing of the Holy Spirit. Discipleship to Christ does not merely result in temporal, earthly blessings—blessings of health, fertility, long life—such as were expected to result from religious devotion. Rather, we are given blessings of the age to come, for the Holy Spirit is our pledge, our down payment and participation in that age to come even here and now. The powers of the age to come are available and active in our lives even now, in this present age.

These blessings are given to us through our sacramental union with Christ as He sits enthroned at the Father's right hand **in the heavenlies**. Through baptism and chrismation, we have been engrafted into Him and made a part of His Body. All that He has accomplished and all that He is, by nature, is now given to us, by grace. Thus we share His death on the Cross, His burial, His Resurrection. The very exaltation with which He has been exalted is given to us. We do not merely sit in the heavenlies along with Christ. Rather (as the untranslatable Greek makes clear), we co-sit with Him at the Father's right hand, exalted with Him far above all earthly authority and power, unreachable by death and harm, invincible in the Son of God.

৵ৎ ৵ৎ ৵ৎ ৵ৎ ৵ৎ

4   even as He chose us in Him before *the* foundation of *the* world, that we should be holy and blameless before Him. In love

5   He predestined us to adoption-as-sons to Himself through Jesus Christ, according to the good-pleasure of His will,

6   to the praise of His glorious grace, with which He graced us in the Beloved.

God's present blessing of us through our union with Christ is consistent with the fact that He **chose us** so that we would be **holy and blameless before Him.** *This* is God's eternal plan for His People

Israel, His plan made **before *the* foundation of *the* world**. It is *not* that His People should be exalted in political preeminence over all the other nations (the preferred and expected hope of many in Zion). Rather, His plan was that His People should **be holy and blameless before Him**. The glory of the Messiah was not that His People should be politically powerful, but that they should be holy. The work of Messiah was not external, but internal; not a change of state, but a change of heart. The divine plan (the "economy" or stewardship, the administration of salvation, as the Fathers called it) was that we should be transformed. We were to be presented "holy and blameless and irreproachable before God" (Col. 1:21), we were to become "faultless and innocent, blameless children of God" (Phil. 2:15). The Messiah came not to exalt Israel to a position of power in the world. Rather, He came in order that we might be "conformed to His image" so that He might be but "the firstborn among many brothers" (Rom. 8:29).

Note: It is *not* that we were "chosen" by God's arbitrary decree from some eternal list of souls, predestined to be saved. The Calvinistic understanding of predestination utterly errs at this point. It is not that we were chosen to be saved while others were chosen to be damned. Rather, it is that we were chosen to **be holy and blameless before Him**. It is not our response to God, but our fate, destiny, and glory which is here under discussion; not our response (either to accept Him and be saved or reject Him and be damned)—rather, the nature of God's salvation. St. Paul's point is *not* that we were chosen (and not rejected). It is that we were chosen *for holiness and blamelessness*, for **adoption** as His true sons.

The divine plan, the fate and glory which God had planned for His foreknown People and for which He **predestined** them before all the ages, was that they should have **adoption-as-sons**. The word in Greek is *uiothesia*—not just "adoption," but "*son*-adoption." Through Jesus Christ and our discipleship to Him, we become not just God's children, but His sons—that is, His heirs (see Rom. 8:17). In Christ, we inherit, with Him, all the vast cosmos and the joy it contains. All that Christ inherits from His Father by right, we share with Him by grace. This is accomplished **according to the**

good-pleasure of His will. The word translated here *good-pleasure* (Gr. *eudokia*) can also be translated "resolve" (thus in 2 Thess. 1:11). It means God's resolve, His decision, the outworking of His will for us in the Gospel. The earthly ministry of Christ—His miracles, His death and Resurrection—this is the divine decision to bless us and make us His sons.

God's salvation in Christ—His making us His holy and blameless sons—is **to the praise of His glorious grace**. The work of the Messiah shows clearly and spectacularly how glorious and abundant is God's grace, His unmerited overflowing favor and love toward us. We tend to take for granted that salvation is by grace, but it was not so self-evident within the context of first-century Judaism. There the emphasis was on earning merit, on acquiring God's goodwill through the piling up of various *mitzvoth* or commandments. But St. Paul here asserts that the outworking of the messianic salvation reveals finally and forever how glorious and triumphant is God's grace. We could do nothing to earn this sonship—we who were utterly condemned to death by our sins. Yet it is freely given to us in Christ nonetheless.

༄ ༄ ༄ ༄ ༄

7   **In Him we have redemption through His Blood, the forgiveness of our offenses, according to the riches of His grace**
8   **which He lavished on us.**

In Jesus, "the Beloved" of the Father (v. 6), we have **redemption through His Blood**. Here is seen the true measure and extent of God's love. Our redemption was to cost nothing less than the precious Blood of Christ. In order to win us back to God from slavery to Satan and sin, Christ had to die, offering His life as a Sacrifice. Yet He did not shrink even from this, in order that we might have **the forgiveness of our offenses**. Note that we are not offered a partial discharge, being put "on parole" (as it were) to God's mercy. Rather, the Blood of Christ purchased our complete pardon, our full forgiveness. Here was the source of the Christian's joy: in a world and society that knew itself guilty and bound by sin, the follower of Jesus knew the peace of being fully forgiven and liberated from the past. This flowed from the generous heart of God, as **the riches of His grace**, which He recklessly and abundantly **lavished on us**. Here is no careful measuring out of the divine pardon, as if God were afraid of being too generous. Rather, the Father pours out His love and favor and grace in a kind of happy and careless abandon, welcoming all the prodigals home to His Table.

ॐ ॐ ॐ ॐ ॐ

8   **In all wisdom and insight**
9   **He made known to us the mystery of His will, according to His good-pleasure which He purposed in Him**
10 **for a stewardship for the fullness of the times, *that is,* the heading-up of all things in Christ, things in the heavens and things on the earth.**

Here we see the intricate and hidden wisdom of the divine Plan. The Gospel comes to us **in all wisdom and insight**—a wisdom not of this age (see 1 Cor. 1:6–8), but of the hidden wisdom of God. This **wisdom** refers to the plan whereby Christ becomes the focal point and source of the new humanity, the New Adam. By His life, death, and Resurrection, Christ became the Font of new life. By being engrafted into Him, men partake of this new life, in which all the categories of this age are transcended, so that there is no longer any "Jew" or "Gentile," but only the new reality of Christ. This is said to be God's **mystery** (Gr. *mysterion*). St. Paul here uses the language of the so-called "mystery religions" of his day. A "mystery," according to this vocabulary, is not something inexplicable. Rather, it is a secret, long hidden from all, but now revealed only to the initiated. Christ is the **mystery** of God—salvation through union with Him (a salvation that transcends all divisions such as "Jew" and "Gentile") was not formerly revealed to any. Though it was prophesied by the Old Testament prophets, its full and true meaning was not understood. Only now, through the apostolic Gospel, is its meaning revealed to the initiated baptized Christians.

St. Paul goes on further to describe this long-hidden **mystery**. It concerns **a stewardship** [Gr. *oikonomia*] **for the fullness of the times**. The Greek term *oikonomia* is difficult to translate and has a history in Orthodox tradition. (As such, it is usually left transliterated as "economy.") Originally it referred to the management of a household (Gr. *oikos*), and thus is sometimes translated "administration" or "stewardship," or sometimes "arrangements." It is this last shade of meaning that predominates here: the divine "economy" is the "arrangements" God made for the salvation of the world through Christ. (In later Orthodox canonical tradition, the term "economy" is used for any pastoral canonical action which helps further these saving "arrangements." For example, when to insist on the strict letter of a rule would harm the believer, the pastor may relax the normative requirement for the sake of the believer's salvation. This change from the norm is called "economy.")

Here St. Paul says that the mystery of Christ is God's divine arrangement for **the fullness of the times**. That is, when the world had been brought to a place of readiness and expectation, Christ came, summing up, uniting, and **heading-up all things** (Gr. *anakephalaio*) in Himself. What is this **heading-up**? It refers to Christ being made the focal point and source of all life. Just as all life in the body, in the thought of the ancients, comes from the head (Gr. *kephale*), so all life in the age to come comes from the Person of Christ. He is constituted the Head over all the world. From Him, from His life, death, Resurrection, and glorification, flow all the life and power in the New Creation. As said above, by divine arrangement, He is the New Adam, the Source of the new and redeemed humanity. Only by being in union with Him is one redeemed and saved. Thus is He said to be the Head over all the cosmos, **things in the heavens and things on the earth**.

ॐ ॐ ॐ ॐ ॐ

ॐ ॐ ॐ ॐ ॐ

10 In Him

11 also we were made an inheritance, having been
predestined according to His purpose who
works all things according to the intention of
His will,

12 so that we who hoped-before in Christ would
be to the praise of His glory.

If Christ is the predestined Source of redemption and renewal
for the age to come, what is the meaning of history up to that point?
What about all that salvation history of Israel? What is the significance of Israel anyway? St. Paul answers: **we** [Jews] **were made an
inheritance**. We were constituted God's People, His prize, His own
possession. St. Paul said before (vv. 5, 6) that God's predestined
plan was that we should be His adopted sons to the praise of His
glorious grace. Here he reiterates that God's predestined plan is that
as His own inheritance, Israel (those who **hoped-before** in Christ
[Gr. *proelpizo*], believing in the Messiah even before He was born)
has no other destiny than to be **to the praise of His glory**. This is
why God has worked through history, intervening, judging, saving,
teaching, and working among the nations **according to the intention of His will**. It is all so that Israel would manifest His glory.

ॐ ॐ ॐ ॐ ॐ

13 In Him, you also, having heard the Word of
truth, the Gospel of your salvation, having also
believed, were sealed in Him with the Holy
Spirit of promise,

14 who is a pledge of our inheritance, for the
redemption of *our* possession, to the praise of
His glory.

The Gentiles also have their part in this divine economy. Israel
is the center and stage of salvation history, but the God of all flesh

has not abandoned the Gentiles either. Having heard the Gospel proclamation, the **Word of truth**, and believed it, they were incorporated into the commonwealth of Israel and included in these divine arrangements.

The inclusion of the Gentiles is described here by St. Paul as their being **sealed** (Gr. *sphragizo*) with the promised **Holy Spirit**. The reference here is a liturgical one. In those days, Christian initiation (or Holy Baptism) consisted of several parts. The new convert, **having believed** and given assent to the Christian Gospel, was stripped of his old garments and then immersed thrice in water in the Name of the Trinity. Having regained his garments, he was anointed, with the laying on of hands, with holy oil. It was through this physical anointing that the inner anointing of the Spirit was given. The newly initiated was then permitted to join the rest of his brethren in the Eucharist and was then fully a member of the Body of Christ. The climax of the initiation itself was the anointing with oil (now called "chrismation") through which the Holy Spirit was given. This anointing was called "the seal" (Gr. *sphragis*). In those days, a seal was used to indicate ownership (and therefore authenticity). St. Paul here says that this baptismal bestowal of the Holy Spirit makes the believers God's own possession, His newly acquired property. For just as a seal marks something as one's own, so God's bestowing of the Spirit marks us as His own.

The gift of the Spirit was **promised**, not just by our Lord Jesus (see John 7:38, 39; 14:16; Luke 24:49) but also by all the prophets. For the crowning hope of the Old Testament was the messianic day when all the children of Israel—even down to the lowest manservant and maidservant—would receive the Spirit once bestowed only on kings and prophets (Joel 2:28, 29). The gift of the Spirit was thus the sum and summit of God's gifts to His children and the proof of their sonship (see Gal. 3:14; 4:6).

More than simply marking us as God's own possession and under His care and protection, the Spirit is given in baptismal chrismation as a **pledge** [Gr. *arrabon*] **of our inheritance**. An *arrabon* is a token given in kind as a down payment, a pledge and promise that one will eventually receive the full payment. For example, if one had purchased a load of flowers, one might be given as an *arrabon* a bouquet of flowers as partial delivery and pledge of receiving the rest. Here the Holy Spirit is given as a pledge of the coming Kingdom, a promise that we will inherit the rest of God's eschatological blessings. For the Spirit is the Person and power of the age to come, and His Presence in our hearts now is a foretaste of that coming age. This pledge of the Spirit is given until we take **possession** of the fullness of the Kingdom on the Last Day. And this is not for our own benefit only, but ultimately to God's glory, **to the praise of His glory**. In the fullness of that Kingdom, God will be all in all.

§III   Opening Prayer—for them to know this glorious salvation (1:15–23)

St. Paul prays that the Father of glory may give the spiritual gift of wisdom to them, so that they may see what glorious things the Father has accomplished for them through Christ. For Christ was raised and exalted above all forever and made the Head over His Body, the Church, so that, as Head and Source, His exalted glory might be given to them.

ॐ ॐ ॐ ॐ ॐ

15 Therefore I *myself* also, having heard of the faith in the Lord Jesus among you and your love for all the saints,

16 do not cease giving thanks for you, making remembrance of you in my prayers;

From his prison in Rome, St. Paul has heard of the spiritual health of the churches of Asia Minor that sprang up through his influence and he overflows with gratitude, **giving thanks** even from his prison. For the apostle has learned the secret of joy: to look not to one's own circumstances, but to the welfare of others as the source of peace and happiness. If they are well in the Lord, he is content. Note that their health consists not only of their **faith in the Lord**

Jesus but also of their **love for all the saints**. Faith and works are not truly sundered one from another: salvation consists of both. Note too this faith and love. Their faith is not just "faith in God"—a generalized and abstract Deity—but especially in **the Lord Jesus**, for without Christ, there is no true Faith. He is the central message of the apostles. Also, their **love** was not narrow, encompassing just those of their own community. True love breaks out, extends past all boundaries. It is directed toward **all the saints**—not just those local ones known to them.

ॐ ॐ ॐ ॐ ॐ

17 that the God of our Lord Jesus Christ, the Father of glory, may give you a spirit of wisdom and of revelation in the real-knowledge of Him,

18 that the eyes of your heart may be enlightened, that you may know what is the hope of His calling, what are the riches of His glorious inheritance in the saints,

19 and what is the surpassing greatness of His power to us who believe, according to the working of His strong might

---

As St. Paul gives thanks for them, he also intercedes for their increased spiritual maturity. (Thus is intercession a natural and inevitable part of life in the Body of Christ: when we think of another, we naturally intercede and pray for that other.) St. Paul's prayer is that **the God** whom they have come to know in **our Lord Jesus Christ** may give them a spiritual gift of revelation. This God is described as **the Father of glory**, not only because He has glorified His Son Jesus, having "seated Him at His right hand in the heavenlies" (v. 20), but also because He will help the Ephesians to see **what are the riches of His glorious inheritance** in them.

The **spirit** referred to here is not the Holy Spirit, but an inner faculty and virtue given by the Holy Spirit. (Thus St. Paul elsewhere says that God "did not give us a spirit of timidity but of power and love and self-control," 2 Tim. 1:7). St. Paul here prays that through the Spirit, they may be given **wisdom**, revealing God to them in all His glory, that they may thus have **real-knowledge** [Gr. *epignosis*] **of Him**. The usual Greek word for "knowledge" is *gnosis*. St. Paul here uses the more precise and intensive word *epignosis*—not just knowledge, but real-knowledge—true, deep, and intimate.

This true knowledge of God, His character, power, and salvation, is perceived with **the eyes of your heart**—not the mind or the head. True spiritual discernment and maturity concerns the heart and will. We need but a tender, simple, and humble heart to know God, not great learning and education.

These are what St. Paul would focus their attention on: the great gifts of hope, riches, and power that God has given to us and this mighty salvation that He has won for us. He would have them know **the hope of His calling**. That is, what wonders, what joy, what glory and blessing await us in the age to come—in the ages of eternity when He will show us "the surpassing riches of His grace in kindness to us" (2:7). Also, he would have them know **the riches of His glorious inheritance in the saints**—that is, what riches we are to inherit, what "weight of glory beyond all comparison" (2 Cor. 4:17). Finally, as he in his apostolic enthusiasm repeats himself for the third time, straining to express in words the inexpressible glory of God given to us, he would have them know **what is the surpassing greatness of His power** to be worked on behalf of us believers. That is, what extraordinary power, beyond all measure and proportion (Gr. *uperballon*), He will exert for us at the final resurrection, changing our corruptible bodies into incorruption.

It is all too easy to take for granted God's gifts. We most easily see the difficulties with which we are surrounded and focus our attention on our sufferings and trials. St. Paul would have them rise above all that. He prays that they be enlightened by the Spirit to see, not the present trials, but the future glory; not our sufferings, but God's gifts laid up for us. By the gift the Spirit gives us, we are to have revealed to us the greatness of our salvation, that we may see and give thanks.

ॐ ॐ ॐ ॐ ॐ

20 which He worked in Christ, when He raised
Him from the dead and seated Him at His right
hand in the heavenlies,
21 far above all rule and authority and power and
dominion, and every name that is named, not
only in this age but also in the coming *age.*
22 And He submitted all things under His feet,
and gave Him *as* Head over all things to the
Church,
23 which is His Body, the fullness of Him who
fills all in all.

All the riches of our salvation which the apostle has described
are given to us only insofar as we are **in Christ**, and united to Him
in sacramental union. God "bared His mighty arm" (Ps. 98:1) and
manifested "His strong might" (v. 19—i.e., His supreme almighti-
ness) through the life, death, and Resurrection of Christ. We
receive and benefit from these mighty acts only when we are part of
His Body, the fullness of Him who fills all in all, united to Him as
to the **Head over all things.** Christ's glorification and exaltation are
described here, but it is *our* glorification and exaltation as well. God
manifested His strength *for us* when He **raised Him from the dead,**
when He **seated Him at His right hand in the heavenlies** so that
He was exalted far above **all rule and power**—not only now, in this
age, but forever. He manifested His strength *for us* when He thus
exalted Christ so that **all things** were **submitted under His feet.**

For this divine glory of the ascended Lord, as **Head over all
things,** is given to us, **His Body,** as well, so that His Church is **the
fullness of Him who fills all in all.** This is what St. Paul means
when he says that God gave Christ *as* **Head over all things to the
Church.** Christ is Head **to the Church** (some translate this *"for* the
Church") because all this heavenly glorification is transmitted and
given to us, even as the Head gives life to the Body. If we would see
the glory that God has stored up for us in the coming ages, we need

only behold Christ, for the glory we shall have *then* is the selfsame glory that the Lord has *now*.

That is why St. Paul says that our salvation (thrice described in verses 18, 19) is **according to . . . His strong might which He worked in Christ** (vv. 19, 20). God has worked our salvation (as it were) *into* Christ. He is our Source, our Head, the Font from which our glorification flows. The glory and life which we will have flow from Him, as life from the Head to the rest of the Body. That is why the Church is described (with apostolic boldness!) as Christ's **fullness**, the overflow of His life and glory—even though He is the One who fills all creation everywhere!

§IV   Their Glorious Salvation (2:1—3:13)

Having prayed for them to know the glory of their salvation (1:15–23), St. Paul now goes on to describe it to them in the chapters to follow (2:1—3:13).

§IV.1   Saved while God's enemies (2:1–10)

> ॐ ॐ ॐ ॐ ॐ
>
> **2** 1 **And you were dead in your offenses and sins,**
> 2 **in which you once walked according to the age of this world, according to the ruler of the authority of the air, of the spirit that is now working in the sons of disobedience.**
> 3 **Among them we *ourselves* also all formerly had our conduct in the desires of our flesh, doing the things willed by the flesh and the mind, and were by nature children of wrath, even as the rest.**

Though translated here as **and you were dead**, this second chapter literally begins, "and you being dead," thus running on immediately without a break from the previous description of the exaltation of Christ in 1:20–23. Christ's mighty salvation for us is seen to be all the more glorious when we reflect how utterly unde-serving we are. St. Paul's attention runs on to the fact that they were not piously awaiting the Messiah. Rather, the Gentiles were com-pletely dead to God, "without hope and without God in the world," "excluded from the life of God because of their hardness of heart" (2:12; 4:18). As idolaters, they walked **according to the age of this world**, living according to the false values of this present evil age. They lived according to Satan, called the **ruler of the authority of the air**. For Satan's demonic hosts fill the air, contaminating it with a spiritual poison, so that all the earthbound must breathe in its lies. Satan is the "god of this world" (2 Cor. 4:4), ruling it as a usurper, actively working in evil men, **the sons of disobedience**.

While the Gentiles were in the thrall of Satan and sin, the Jews too, though awaiting the Messiah in hope, were also shackled by sin. **We** *ourselves* **also**, St. Paul wrote, classing himself and his fellow-Jews along with the Gentiles, **were by nature**, in their inmost be-ings, **children of wrath**, deserving the severity of the Divine Judg-ment. For though the Law could teach them what was right, it could not liberate them and empower them actually to do it. Thus, along with their Gentile comrades, they too lived in slavery to **the desires of** the **flesh**. Whatever was dictated and **willed by the flesh and the mind**, that was what they obediently did. Whatever appetites, impulses, compulsions, or obsessions sprang from the inflamed body or the disordered mind—whatever fantasies or desires made them-selves known, that was the directive they followed. Not only sexual desires either, but any consuming desire—whether of anger, resent-ment, envy, gluttony, greed, sulkiness, pride, coldness of heart. The lower nature, in all its depressing variety, ruled them.

శ్రీ శ్రీ శ్రీ శ్రీ శ్రీ

4   But God, rich in mercy, because of His great
    love with which He loved us,
5   even when we were dead in our offenses, co-
    quickened us with Christ (by grace you have
    been saved),

> 6   and co-raised us up with Him, and co-seated
>   us with Him in the heavenlies in Christ Jesus,
> 7   so that in the ages to come He might show the
>   surpassing riches of His grace in kindness to-
>   ward us in Christ Jesus.

Here we have a revelation of the inner heart of our God. Despite our wretchedness, our inner coldness which rebels against His Love, God still loves us. Though He hates sin and "has indignation every day" (Ps. 7:11), yet in His love He "could not endure to behold mankind oppressed by the devil" (prayer for the blessing of baptismal water). He is **rich in mercy**, fabulously overflowing with compassion. When He saw us **dead in our offenses** (spiritual suicides, all of us), He gave us life, by uniting us to His Christ so that we share His Resurrection and His sitting at the Father's right hand **in the heavenlies**. The verbs here do not translate well into melodious English. St. Paul does not write that God "made us alive" or that He "raised us" or "seated us" in the heavenlies. Rather, he writes that God **co-quickened us, co-raised us, co-seated us** with Christ. The Greek verbs are *suzoopoieo, sunegeiro, sugkathizo*. The *su-* prefix in the Greek indicates a "co-" element in the verb. The thought is that, through our baptismal union with Christ, we share His own life, His own Resurrection, His own sitting at the Father's right hand. Not that we will be raised as Christ was, but that we share His own Resurrection, so that we were raised *with Christ*. As we are incorporated members of His Body, these powers that are in Him—this new life, His crucifixion death to sin, His burial, Resurrection, Ascension, heavenly glory at the Father's right hand—all these powers are now at work in us, through our baptismal union with Him. And since our baptism was not earned, but freely given, it is described as being saved **by grace**.

Here we see the generosity of our God, the boundless burning love He has for us. Though we were dead to Him, He saved us by grace so that in the eternal ages to come He might further **show the surpassing riches of His grace in kindness toward us**. Once again the apostolic focus is not on this vale of tears, but on the sunlit land of our eternal reward. "We look to the things which are eternal" (2 Cor. 4:18) and behold the limitless riches of His grace, a kindness and a glory bestowed on us that beggars description.

ॐ ॐ ॐ ॐ ॐ

8   For by grace you have been saved through faith; and this *is* not of yourselves, *it is* the gift of God;
9   not of works, so that no one may boast.
10 For we are His workmanship, created in Christ Jesus for good works, which God prearranged so that we would walk in them.

Having described God's plan for us, St. Paul steps back to reflect and theologize on it. Though our salvation is of course the result of our **faith**—our repentant response to God and our discipleship to Jesus—it is not our own heroic accomplishment. Our rescue is not **of yourselves**—not the result of any inner triumph, not the manifestation of any goodness found in ourselves. The Pharisaical Jewish understanding of our relationship with God was based on **works**—the acquiring and piling up of various *mitzvoth* or commandments. Reward and blessing were based on the successful struggle to accomplish the will of God, to keep His external demands, to "measure up," to acquire merit. In contrast to all this, St. Paul declares with amazement that we are saved **by grace**, as the undeserved **gift of God**. We emerged from our baptismal initiation as the blameless sons of God, united to Christ, sharing His glory—all this despite our not having done any great feat worthy of blessing. Rather, we approached the font as condemned sinners, "by nature children of wrath" (v. 3). Yet we emerged as united to the Messiah, seated in the heavenlies, "far above all rule, authority, power, and dominion" (1:21). Thus, we have no grounds to **boast**, exalting ourselves one over the other, puffing ourselves up in the presence of God. Humility, the foundation of all Orthodox spirituality, is thus built into our Faith, as flowing from the baptismal experience itself.

Far from being self-made, we are the **workmanship** and handiwork of God. He has recreated us as His new creation **in Christ Jesus**. He fashioned us afresh, making us anew. And as no man can take credit for his own creation, so none of us can boast of our new life, status, or glory. It is entirely the work of God.

God created us, not for our own pleasure, not to pursue our own ends and destinies, but to glorify Him. That is, **for good works**. Note that good works are inseparable from the Christian life, and no one can be saved without them. Not, however, that the good works are the ground and cause of our salvation—for St. Paul has just said that our salvation is **not of works**. But rather, good works are what the Christian life is all about. God has **prearranged that we would walk in them**. This means that before this age, from all eternity, God had planned that we should be resplendent with the light of kindness and love. It is a part of what St. Paul has already said about our predestination. God's predestined plan was that His People should be "conformed to the image of His Son" (Rom. 8:29), being, like Him, "holy and blameless" (1:4). Here is the practical outworking of this conformity in holiness—that we walk in good works. These works are said to be **prearranged** because the holy and blameless life in which they are performed is part of the predestined plan of God for us. "To be conformed to the image of His Son" (Rom. 8:29) means not only our glorification in the age to come; it also means "shining as lights in the world" (Phil. 2:15) now.

§IV.2   Saved while wtrangers to God's covenant (2:11–22)

$$❧ ❧ ❧ ❧ ❧$$

11 Therefore remember that once you *yourselves*, the Gentiles in the flesh, who are called "*the* Uncircumcision" by what is called "*the* Circumcision" (which is *made* in the flesh, made-with-hands)—

12 *remember* that you were at that time separate from Christ, estranged from the citizenship of

> Israel, and strangers to the covenants of promise, not having *any* hope and without-God in the world.

Having explained what great things God has done for them in Christ (saving them by incorporation into Christ, even when they were God's enemies), St. Paul continues to press the contrast of their former Gentile life with their present privileges in the Church. For gratitude (and its result, thanksgiving) is the sum of our offering to God, and gratitude can best flourish in our hearts when we remember our former state and from what God has rescued us. Familiarity with God's grace can make us forget too easily the wonder of our salvation. Thus we are called to **remember** our former plight in order to see our life in the Church as the miracle it is.

The usual term of abuse used by the Jews for the Gentiles was "the Uncircumcised." The spirit of the term is aptly reflected in its use by David, when he said, "Who is this uncircumcised Philistine that he should defy the armies of the Living God?" (1 Sam. 17:26). To stigmatize the Gentiles as the Uncircumcision was to denounce them as barbaric, stupid, insensitive, devoid of God's grace. Thus St. Paul is careful to say **you . . . Gentiles in the flesh** [i.e. by birth], **who are** commonly **called "*the* Uncircumcision"**—by the Jews, but not now, by St. Paul.

In saying that the Gentiles are stigmatized as uncircumcised by the Jews, he refers to the Jews as those who delight to boast of themselves as **the Circumcision**. But he immediately strikes out at this much-vaunted circumcision in which his Jewish compatriots boasted. He himself stigmatizes it as merely *made* **in the flesh**. In itself, he says, it is nothing spiritual, but a mere surgical operation. Without faithfulness to God, it avails no more than any other surgical act (see Rom. 2:28, 29). He also, in a bold word, describes Jewish circumcision as **made-with-hands** (Gr. *cheiropoietos*). This is quite radical, because this word is the one usually used in Jewish polemics to describe Gentile idols and shrines. The Jews scorned the idols of the Gentiles as vain, useless, not true divinities but merely made by the hands of men. The Gentiles' idols were mere "silver and gold, the work of men's hands" (Ps. 115:4); the God who made the world "does not live in shrines made with hands" (Acts 17:24). St. Paul takes this term and applies it here to the rite of circumcision itself. In so doing, he utterly distances himself from the Jewish condemnation of the Gentiles and from their boasting of their special status as the Circumcised.

Though far from narrow Jewish triumphalism, St. Paul nonetheless reminds his Gentile hearers of their former plight. They were **separate from Christ**. They did not await the Messiah, had no relation to Him nor right to His mercy. Unlike **the citizenship** and holy nation **of Israel**, they were not kept under God's protection and care, awaiting His coming salvation and the time when Christ would bring in the Kingdom. They were, in fact, utter **strangers to the covenants of promise**. Though the Covenant with God promised good things to Israel, they were entitled to none of them. They did not have *any* **hope**. They had no grounds for thinking the coming Kingdom, promised to the Jews, would benefit them. They were alone, adrift in the world, without help or rescue, uncared-for, forgotten: **without-God** [Gr. *atheos*] **in the world**.

ॐ ॐ ॐ ॐ ॐ

13 But now in Christ Jesus you who were once "far off" have become "near" in the Blood of Christ.

14 For He *Himself* is our peace, who made *us* both into one, having destroyed the dividing middle-wall

15 *of* the enmity, abolishing in His flesh the Law of commandments *contained* in decrees, so that in Himself He might create the two into one new man, making peace,

16 and might reconcile *us* both in one body to God through the Cross, having killed the enmity by it.

17 And having come, He preached peace to you who

> were far off and peace to those who were near;
> 18 for through Him we both have access in one
> Spirit to the Father.

In verse 13, St. Paul alludes to the prophecy of Isaiah 57:19: "Peace, peace to the far and to the near, says Yahweh, and I will heal him." In its original context, this prophecy referred to the restoration of those Jews near at hand and also of the far-flung Jewish exiles. St. Paul here applies it to the final messianic salvation in Christ, wherein those who are **near** are the Jews and those **far off** are the Gentiles. The Gentiles, he says, formerly "without God in the world" (v. 12), have **become "near,"** united to the commonwealth of Israel.

How has this happened? Through the Blood of Christ, His saving death on the life-giving Cross. For the Cross brings forgiveness to the Gentiles, even though they never knew nor concerned themselves with **the Law of commandments**, with its minute and multitudinous **decrees** and rules. The gracious forgiveness of God bypassed and transcended this Law, making it irrelevant to salvation. The new humanity, the new creation that flows from sacramental union with Christ, is offered to all, whether Jew or Gentile. Thus His Cross is said to have **destroyed the dividing middle-wall** *of* **the enmity** that from time immemorial divided Jew from Gentile. By offering Himself as saving and sanctifying Sacrifice, the Lord is said to have **abolished in His flesh** the hostility and division of Jew and Gentile, for the same Life is given to both. The two groups have now been made **into one**; the categories of Jew and Gentile have been transcended so that both Jews and Gentiles are now **one new man**—neither Jew nor Gentile, but "a new creation" (Gal. 6:15). For the Law was what characterized the Jew and made him different from the Gentile. This Law has been rendered irrelevant to salvation. Both now enjoy access to God the Father **in one** and the same **Spirit**, finding forgiveness through **one** and the same **body** sacrificed on the Cross. Thus they find themselves **reconciled** in that Body, **the enmity** between them having been **killed** through the Cross. Christ is the **peace** between all men.

Having come, He preached peace, both to those **far off** and
those **near**. Once again, in verse 17, the reference to those **far off**
and **near** is from Isaiah 57:19. The Lord came, during His earthly
ministry, bringing the Good News of peace and reconciliation with
God (the word here translated *preach* [Gr. *evaggelizo*] is usually rendered "to bring Good News"). In His preaching, this Kingdom was
not just offered to respectable Jews, but also to any who sought for
God with an open and penitent heart—even disreputable sinners,
so that there was hope also for the Gentiles (see Luke 14:15–24;
Matt. 21:33–44). It was these Gentiles who now had **access**, with
their Jewish brothers, to **the Father** of them all **in one Spirit**.

The term **in one Spirit** refers here primarily to the eucharistic
assembly. For the issue here is one of access—how do we approach
the awe-inspiring Throne, before which angels and archangels veil
their faces and which they tremble to approach? How do we sinners, wretches who "drink iniquity like water" (Job 15:16), dare to
address the heavenly God as **Father**? This access and boldness is
given us only through the Cross of Christ, His one and unrepeatable
Sacrifice. It is this Sacrifice that the Spirit makes present in our
eucharistic memorial. Everything in the Divine Liturgy is accomplished in the Spirit. The *epiclesis* (the invocation of the Spirit
during the Anaphora) only sums up and expresses the charismatic quality of *all* our worship, as it calls down the Holy Spirit
"upon us and upon these Gifts [of Bread and Wine] here offered."
All of our approach to God—at all times—is accomplished in the
Spirit.

ॐ ॐ ॐ ॐ ॐ

19 So then you are no longer strangers and sojour-
    ners, but co-citizens with the saints, and
    housemates of God,

20 having been built-up on the foundation of the
    apostles and prophets, Christ Jesus Himself
    being the cornerstone,

21 in whom the whole building, being co-joined,

> grows into a holy sanctuary in *the* Lord,
> 22 in whom you also are being co-built into a dwelling-place of God in *the* Spirit.

The Gentiles were formerly **strangers and sojourners** (Gr. *xenoi kai paroikoi*). The image is of a foreigner visiting the land of Israel, having no fixed or permanent place there, living *beside* their homes (*para oikos*—the original meaning of *paroikos*, "sojourner"), but not *with* them. They had no true place there. They did not belong to the Chosen People and experienced all the instability and vulnerability of those who lived on the fringes of ordered society in those days. Such was the spiritual position of the Gentiles to whom St. Paul wrote. Now, however, through the Cross, they have been brought near and are **co-citizens with the saints**—with Abraham, Isaac, and Jacob, with David, Solomon, and the prophets. The salvation history of Israel is now *their* history too, and the promises made to the patriarchs and their descendants belong to them as well. More than this, they are described as **housemates of God** (Gr. *oiketoi tou Theou*), dwelling with God in His household (Gr. *oikos*). Formerly, they were outsiders. Now they are family.

St. Paul uses the image of the Church as sacred temple. For even as, in the ancient world, a deity would dwell within a temple, so now the Lord indwells His People, manifesting His Presence when but "two or three would gather in His Name" at their eucharistic assembly (Matt. 18:20). This living temple (in which each stone is a disciple of Jesus) is built upon the foundation of **the apostles and prophets**. The reference is to the apostles and prophets of the New Testament dispensation (such as St. Paul refers to elsewhere in this epistle, e.g. 4:11) and not to the prophets of the Old Testament. Those New Testament prophets were quite prominent in the early days. St. Paul was sent out on his original apostolic mission, along with St. Barnabas, by the word of the prophets at Antioch (Acts 13:1–3). Prophets in every Christian community (such as Agabus) prophesied concerning St. Paul's imprisonment (Acts 20:23; 21:11). As late as the close of the first century, prophets were still prominent—so much so that the *Didache* (a Church "handbook"

dating from Syria around AD 100) had to deal with potential problems that might arise from their ministry.

Here St. Paul says that they, along with the apostles, constitute
the foundation of the Church. That is, the Church is built upon the
authoritative historical witness to Jesus (such as is given by the
apostles) and the work and presence of the Holy Spirit (such as is
manifested, for example, by the prophets). The Church then is a
combination of the historical and the charismatic, rooted both in
the first century and in the Kingdom. A foundation, of course, is
only laid once. Thus the apostles are no more. They have given
their historical witness to Jesus and His Resurrection (see Acts 1:21,
22) and been gathered to their fathers. There can, by definition, be
no more apostles—nor is their continuation required, for the foundation has been laid once-for-all. Similarly, the prophets, as they
existed in those early days, are seen no more in the historic Church.
Nonetheless, the spiritual powers and realities manifested by them
continue, for apostolicity and prophecy are the Lord's abiding gifts
to His Church. The witness of the apostles continues in their deposit of the Faith (of which the New Testament Scriptures are the
crown). The work and presence of the Spirit also continues in the
Church, manifested through holy men and women (one thinks of
such "prophetic" persons as St. Seraphim of Sarov). This double
reality of apostolic witness and prophetic power forms the sure foundation on which the Church is built.

The image of **Christ Jesus** as the **cornerstone** reflects our Lord's
own usage of Psalm 118:22 (see Matt. 21:42). The Messiah of the
House of David, rejected as worthless by the world, turns out by the
Providence of God to be the most valuable and pivotal Stone. Like a
cornerstone, the Lord's Presence holds together all else in the Church.

The assembled gathering of believers **grows into a holy sanctu-
ary**. That is, the Lord continually manifests His Presence among
them, as a deity dwells within a temple shrine. Through the Divine
Liturgy, by the power of the **Spirit**, the Presence of Christ is felt,
His power experienced, His transforming love revealed. This happens
as the believers are **co-joined** (Gr. *sunarmologeo*) and **co-built**

(Gr. *sunoikomeo*). Once again, the Greek prefix *sun-* expresses the idea of being *jointly* compacted, of a corporate bond. This bond, which holds the Church together so that it grows into a temple manifesting the indwelling Lord, is love (see 4:16; Col. 3:14). Without love for one another, no spiritual growth is possible in the Church, nor can the indwelling fullness of the Lord be seen. With love for one another, the assembled gathering of believers is experienced as **a dwelling-place of God**—a place where the Most High God makes His home.

§IV.3   Paul now their servant of this mystery of salvation (3:1–13)

> ॐ ॐ ॐ ॐ ॐ
>
> **3** 1   For this reason, I *myself,* Paul, the prisoner of Christ Jesus for you Gentiles—

St. Paul was, of course, a **prisoner** of Rome. His freedom, his life, his fate were all in the hands of Rome—of the Roman jailers and judges. Yet St. Paul did not see it that way. He knew that his true fate—whether for freedom or incarceration, for life or death— lay with his **Christ Jesus.** So it is with us in our lives. We may think of ourselves as at the mercy of external, secular forces, whether economic or governmental. Yet we, like St. Paul before us, are in the hands of God.

The apostle did not write his epistles himself. His usual custom was to dictate them to a secretary who would write down what he said (see Rom. 16:22, where his secretary Tertius adds his own greetings). So here, he begins to dictate a prayer for them. He begins to write, **For this reason, I *myself,* Paul, the prisoner of Christ Jesus for you Gentiles,** bend my knees before the Father . . . (see 3:14). But the expression **for you Gentiles** catches at his heart and he begins a long digression (3:2–13) about his ministry to the Gentiles and his apostolic insight into their inclusion into Christ.

ॐ ॐ ॐ ॐ ॐ

2   if indeed you have heard of the stewardship of
    God's grace which was given to me for you;

3   how the mystery was made known to me by a
    revelation, as I wrote-before in brief.

4   When you read this you can understand my
    insight into the mystery of Christ,

5   which in other generations was not made
    known to the sons of men, as it has been
    revealed now to His holy apostles and proph-
    ets in the Spirit;

6   *that is*, how the Gentiles are joint-heirs and a
    joint-body, and joint-partakers of the promise
    in Christ Jesus through the Gospel,

He begins in verse 1 by mentioning his ministry **for you Gentiles** and then breaks off, saying, "Surely you have heard about my ministry!" This ministry he refers to as **the stewardship of God's grace which was given to me for you**. The word here translated *stewardship* is the Greek word *oikonomia*. The word is of some elasticity. The steward (Gr. *oikonomos*) of one's house was, in those days, the man entrusted with all the arrangements and administration of the affairs of the house (Gr. *oikos*). St. Paul describes his ministry as one of such stewardship. The steward actually owned nothing in the house, but was entrusted by the master with care and use of it all. He was required to spend the household's money to pay the bills and to keep things running smoothly. Though owning nothing himself, he actually possessed authority, in his master's name, over everything. St. Paul, as God's steward, governs the Church, making available **God's grace** through the Gospel. This ministry is not given for his own benefit or self-aggrandizement, but **for you**—the Gentiles to whom he preaches.

So it is with all authentic Christian ministry. Those in Holy Orders are not to use their ministries solely for their own benefit. They are ordained for the sake of others. The Church and its priesthood do not belong to them, but to their Master. Theirs is but a stewardship—for which they will have to give an account to their Lord on the Last Day.

St. Paul received his **revelation** of Christ's Gospel on the road to Damascus, when the Lord appeared to him (Acts 9:1–19). This Gospel he calls **the mystery** (Gr. *musterion*). A "mystery" was not something that defied understanding, as in our modern definition of that word. Rather, a *musterion* was something which had been hidden for ages and was now revealed only to the initiated few. The Gospel, St. Paul says, was not revealed to the sons of men before. Only now, through the **holy apostles and prophets** of the Church, has it been **revealed . . . in the Spirit.**

What is the content of this **mystery?** That the Gentiles, formerly estranged from God and His Chosen People, are now **joint-heirs** (Gr. *sugkleronoma*), a **joint-body** (Gr. *sussoma*) and **joint-partakers** (Gr. *summetoxa*) of the divine promises of salvation. As he **wrote-before** in the earlier part of this letter (2:1–22), there is now a New Creation, a "new man" (2:15), transcending both Jew and Gentile. It is this aspect of the Gospel which is new in the earth. That the Gentiles will one day worship the God of Israel alongside the Jews is nothing new (see Is. 2:1–4). What *is* new is this manifestation of a New Humanity, one in which the earthly categories of Jew and Gentile will be utterly swept away.

ॐ ॐ ॐ ॐ ॐ

7   of which I became a servant, according to the gift of God's grace which was given to me according to the working of His power.

8   To me, the very least of all saints, this grace was given, to preach to the Gentiles the unsearchable riches of Christ,

---

St. Paul continues to describe his stewardship—and the moral authority through which he addresses his audience. He is but **a servant** of God. As is his wont, St. Paul directs attention away from himself and toward his Lord. What he has been able to accomplish is not due to any greatness of his own. Rather, as a mere **servant**, he owes it all to **the gift of God's grace**. All his apostolic miracles (see Acts 14:3; 2 Cor. 12:12), the many conversions he has made, all his countless works—all these he ascribes to **the working of** God's **power**. Paul himself is but **the very least of all saints**. The word he uses here to describe himself is the Greek word *elaxistotero*, meaning "trivial, unimportant," literally "less than the least." St. Paul is not here indulging in any false modesty—which so often masks an overweaning and secret pride. Rather, he could never forget that he was not fit even to be called an apostle "because I persecuted the Church of God" (1 Cor. 15:9). (In his dreams, did the countenance of St. Stephen the Protomartyr appear to him, shining like an angel of God, as Paul held the coats of his murderers? see Acts 6:15; 7:54–60.) It is not that he is hag-ridden or tormented by his past, but he uses his past sins to maintain humility before God.

ॐ ॐ ॐ ॐ ॐ

9 and to enlighten all as to what is the stewardship of the mystery which for ages has been hidden in God who created all things;

10 so that the manifold wisdom of God might now be made known through the Church to the rulers and the authorities in the heavenlies.

11 This was according to the purpose of the ages which He made in Christ Jesus our Lord,

12 in whom we have boldness and confidence of access through faith in Him.

13 Therefore I ask you not to lose heart at my tribulations for you, which are your glory.

Though himself insignificant, he was given apostolic grace to announce to the nations the good news (Gr. *evaggelizo*, "to preach the Gospel") of the "unsearchable riches of Christ" (v. 8) and to **enlighten** them, proclaiming to them the **stewardship**

(Gr. *oikonomia*) or divine plan of the Gospel *musterion*.

Building on his earlier description of the Gospel as unknown in previous generations (v. 5), St. Paul describes the Gospel he proclaims as **the mystery which for ages has been hidden in God**. Its open proclamation to all now is **according to the purpose of the ages**. That is, all history has been leading up to this time. The Christian movement is no mere sociological fad, no accident, explainable in terms of the religious and social trends and pressures of the time. Rather, it is the end and goal to which all the previous ages have been leading. All world history has been a preparation for this. Now the time is ripe for the revelation of what has long lain **hidden in God**, awaiting its proper time. Though himself small and insignificant, St. Paul knows himself called to play a part in the true destiny of the world. He knows that upon himself and his generation "the end and goal of the ages has come" (1 Cor. 10:11). His true dignity lies not in his own worth, but in that he is called to play a part in this cosmic drama.

This is what the ages have been leading up to—this revelation of God's hidden wisdom. St. Paul describes this wisdom as **manifold** (Gr. *polupoikilos*)—literally, "many-sided" (see the use of *poikilos* in the LXX for Joseph's coat of many colors, Gen. 37:4). That is, God in His Providence knits together all causes, events, and human decisions to fulfill His own purposes for our salvation. All the intricacies of our human condition, all the complicated recesses of the human heart with all its sorrow, sickness, and need, are answered and met in Christ.

St. Paul also says that this wisdom is **made known through the Church to the rulers and the authorities in the heavenlies**. The Gospel he proclaims is not only eternal and age-long in its preparation. It is also cosmic in its scope. It concerns not only the children of men on earth, but also the angelic powers **in the heavenlies**—both unfallen and fallen. For the whole cosmos has been disrupted by sin, both "things on earth and in heaven" (Col. 1:20). Not only are there wars upon the earth, but there is war in heaven also, with Satan's fallen angels fighting against God and taking His creation captive. These demonic **rulers and authorities** now are made to acknowledge God's wisdom and victory, having been "disarmed and triumphed over by the Cross" (Col. 2:15). Thus the holy angels also, our comrades in the struggle, see with amazement the victory of their God, beholding now the mysteries into which they before "longed to look" (1 Pet. 1:12). What is being accomplished **through the Church** is no passing fad, no "movement" which will enjoy popularity before it fades forever. Rather, it is the eschatological destiny of the cosmos, the goal of the ages and the hope of all.

Before this Gospel came upon the earth, sinful man had no sure **access** (Gr. *prosagoge*—literally, "to go towards") into the Divine Presence. All religious rites of sacrifice expressed the desire for such access and union with God, but none could accomplish it. The best of them—the sacrifices of Judaism—were but a prophecy and pledge. They could express the desire, but could not fulfill it, for it was impossible that "the blood of bulls and goats should take away sins" (Heb. 10:4). Now, through the Christ proclaimed by the Church, even we sinners **have boldness** to approach God and have union with Him. He is the fulfillment of all religion, for His once-for-all Sacrifice accomplished what all religion vainly attempted to do. Appearing now "at the end of the age," Christ has "put away sin by the Sacrifice of Himself" (Heb. 9:26).

Though St. Paul is a prisoner (3:1) and suffers as such, they are not to lose heart over this. It is natural for them, seeing their leader suffering for the Faith, to become fearful that they are next! And what will this catastrophic setback mean for the Church? Perhaps they should be ashamed to admit they are part of this movement! On the contrary, says St. Paul, my tribulations are your glory. Suffering endured for Christ is no disaster, but a crown and adornment. That their apostolic leader is thus honored by suffering for the Lord is their boast before angels and men.

§V Prayer for Them to Mature into the Love of Christ (3:14–21)

ॐ ॐ ॐ ॐ ॐ

༄ ༄ ༄ ༄ ༄

14 Therefore I bend my knees before the Father,
15 from whom every family in *the* heavens and
   on earth is named,

St. Paul now returns to the prayer he began in 3:1. It was a prayer uttered with the deepest feeling, for in praying, he **bends** his **knees**. The normal posture for prayer was standing, not kneeling. One only knelt when one felt overwhelmed, driven to one's knees by emotion. Thus did our Lord pray on His knees in Gethsemane (Luke 22:41). Thus did St. Paul pray on his knees when taking leave of his beloved Ephesian presbyters for the last time before his arrest, knowing that he would see them no more (Acts 20:36–38). It often expressed sorrow—for which reason the Church, in her canons, forbids kneeling on Sundays and during the Paschal season, for these are times of joy.

St. Paul here uses a play on words not easily translated into English. Every **family** (Gr. *patria*) is a family, in the thought of the ancients, because it is headed by a father (Gr. *pater*). All such "fatherhoods," St. Paul says, find their ultimate source in God, the Father of all. He is the true Head of all, the true Source of life for all—whether angels **in *the* heavens** or people **on earth**. We may look to our own human fathers as authorities, as the sources of our life, but God is our ultimate Source. So it is that we look to Him to give us life, to be "strengthened with power . . . in the inner man" (v. 16).

༄ ༄ ༄ ༄ ༄

16 that He would give you, according to the riches
   of His glory, to be strengthened with power
   through His Spirit in the inner man,
17 that Christ may dwell in your hearts through
   faith; and that you, being rooted and founded
   in love,

> 18 may have strength *enough* to grasp with all the
> saints what is the breadth and length and height
> and depth,
> 19 and to know the love of Christ which surpasses
> knowledge, that you may be filled with all the
> fullness of God.

St. Paul prays that they may mature into the love of Christ. Specifically, he prays that they may be **strengthened with power through His Spirit**. The word *power* (Gr. *dunamis*) is the word often associated with the action of the Holy Spirit. The Lord, for example, promised His Apostles that they would receive "power" (*dunamis*) when the Holy Spirit came upon them (Acts 1:8). The magnitude of this strength for which St. Paul here prays may be measured by **the riches of** God's **glory**. Thus it is no minor support, no little extra help supplementing their own resources. Rather, what is expected is a continuous transformation, an ongoing *theosis* or partaking of the divine nature (see 2 Pet. 1:4), going "from glory to glory" (2 Cor. 3:18). The Spirit is to lead them in the continuing process of Christian maturity, so that Christ is increasingly to **dwell** [Gr. *katoikeo*] **in your hearts**. That is, the Lord is to more and more make Himself a home (Gr. *oikos*) within them. As He promised His disciples, He and His Father will come "and make their abode" in them (John 14:23).

What is the nature of this maturity for which St. Paul prays?

1. It is **through faith**. That is, it does not happen automatically, but only through their ongoing relationship of discipleship and obedience to Christ.

2. It is **rooted and founded in love**. The word here translated *founded* (Gr. *themelioo*) comes from the word for "foundation" (Gr. *themelios*). St. Paul here tells us that love is the spiritual foundation for everything in our Christian life, and that it is only through love that we are **rooted** and have security. If we do not love, we are not spiritually secured and can be easily blown away.

3. It consists of being enabled by God **to grasp with all the saints** the full **love of Christ** so that at last we are **filled with all the**

fullness of God. St. Paul strains at the limits of language and grammar to express this **love of Christ**, which **surpasses knowledge**, overwhelming and dwarfing with its immensity the puny capabilities and intellects of men.

His prayer is that they might **have strength *enough*** [Gr. *exisxuo*, a more intensive verb than *isxuo*, "to have strength"] **to grasp . . . what is the breadth and length and height and depth** of Christ's love, revealed in His Gospel. Strength for such a revelation can only come as God's gift. St. Paul here seems to look around at all the boundless, limitless universe—up and down, from east to west—and to see in the vastness of the world an image of the vastness of Christ's love. As the Psalmist sang, "As far as the east is from the west, so far does He remove our transgressions from us" (Ps. 103:12). St. Paul here too is overcome by the magnitude of the Savior's love. (Some Fathers, such as St. Augustine, also saw in this verse an image of the Cross. Even as the Cross has four directions—as it stretches crosswise, having breadth and length, and vertically, having height and depth—just so does it reveal the boundless love of Christ.)

Such love is to be comprehended **with all the saints**—that is, in community, as a part of the Church. God's love cannot be **known** and experienced in isolation. Christianity is a corporate faith, and salvation comes to us as we are part of a family. It is as we work out our salvation with our brothers and sisters, praying for them, suffering with them, serving them, worshipping with them as part of one eucharistic Body, that we are enabled to **grasp** and **know** this love of Christ.

4. Finally, it finds its climax in our being **filled with all the fullness of God**. This is the goal of our Christian life, the true maturity—to reach "the measure of the stature of the fullness of Christ" (Eph. 4:13). Our goal is not simply to be forgiven, to "get to heaven." Glorious as this is, the manifold wisdom of God has more for us. His plan is that we should be filled with all His own fullness, to be filled as God is full. This is what is finally meant by being partakers of the divine nature (2 Pet. 1:4), or *theosis*, and of being conformed to the image of Christ so that He is the firstborn of many brothers

(Rom. 8:29). While still and forever remaining finite and created, we are even so to be glorified with the divine glory. Thus the Fathers did not shrink from saying, "God became Man so that man could become God."

ॐ   ॐ   ॐ   ॐ   ॐ

20 Now to Him who is able to do far more abun-
     dantly beyond all that we ask or understand,
     according to the power working among us,
21 to Him be the glory in the Church *and* in
     Christ Jesus to all the generations of the ages
     of ages. Amen.

St. Paul concludes his prayer with a typically Jewish doxology, ascribing glory to God. God is here described as being **able to do far more abundantly beyond all that we ask or understand**. Having described our salvation, maturity, and spiritual goal in such superlative terms (vv. 16–19), he is overwhelmed at the power of God. Who would have dared **ask** for or even think of such amazing things? No one on earth would dare to hope for such a love and such a salvation. Yet God has done such things for us in Christ. For this **power** and salvation even now are **working among us**. We are the proof of such amazing and mind-boggling love.

So it is that St. Paul ascribes **glory** to Him, **to all the generations of the ages of ages**. And note finally where God's glory is eternally manifested. It is **in the Church *and* in Christ Jesus**. The two, the Lord and His Church, are here paired, as if they are one reality. For so they are in the Gospel mystery, the Church being "the Body and Fullness of Him who fills all in all" (Eph. 1:23). The Church is now and ever inseparable from her Lord. So it is that God's glory is eternally seen in Christ—both in the Incarnate Lord and in us, His Body.

ॐ   ॐ   ॐ   ॐ   ॐ

§VI   Exhortation to Mature into the Love of Christ (4:1—6:9)

§VI.1   Maturity of unity (4:1–16)

ॐ ॐ ॐ ॐ ॐ

4 1   Therefore I *myself*, the prisoner of *the* Lord, encourage you to walk worthy of the calling to which you have been called,

2   with all humility and meekness, with patience, bearing with one another in love,

3   being eager to keep the unity of the Spirit in the bond of peace.

As before St. Paul prayed for them to know the glory of their salvation (1:15–23) and then wrote to describe this glory (2:1–22), so here he follows up his prayer for them to mature in love (3:14–21) with a description of that maturity for which he has prayed. He draws upon his moral authority as **the prisoner of *the* Lord** and one who is suffering for Him (the **I** is emphatic in the Greek) as he **encourages** them to **walk worthy** of their baptismal **calling**.

In baptism, we were **called** to be saints, adopted as the sons and heirs of God (see Eph. 1:5) so that we now dare to address the heavenly God as "Father." Since we were called out of our old life into such privilege and holiness, we must strive to live in holiness. "As He who called you is holy," writes St. Peter, "be holy yourselves in all your conduct" (2 Pet. 1:15).

This life of holiness is described by St. Paul as being characterized by **humility, meekness, patience**, and loving forbearance.

First the apostle exhorts us to **humility** (Gr. *tapeinophrosune*). Originally in secular Greek, this word had a negative connotation, being synonymous with cringing servility, disgrace, slavishness. It was the Christian Faith that rescued this word from such bad company and turned it into one of the virtues. This is because we see what true humility is like—that it does not have to be cringing and contemptible. We see the humility of the Son of God, who humbled Himself for our sake, leaving the glory of the high halls of heaven for the desolation of the Cross. We see the humility that is stronger than the pride of men. We see that even in the purple of mockery before Pilate, even from the darkness of Golgotha, the divine humility shines like the sun, illumining all the earth, revealing our strutting pride to be the puny and pathetic thing it is. Thereafter, all His followers know themselves called to this same saving humility, in which is contained the power of God.

The next word St. Paul uses is **meekness** (Gr. *praotetos*). Once again, the world fundamentally misunderstands meekness and confuses it with the pathetic weakness of the oppressed who dare not protest. But meekness is not about lack of strength; it is about self-control. The man who lacks meekness is not strong. Rather, he is at the mercy of his passions and his temper. The meek man has power over his passions and control over his strength. The word is used in secular Greek for animals that have been trained and domesticated. The trained lion, the guard dog, has *praotetos*. It does not run wild. Its strength is under control. This is a characteristic of the Christian who walks worthy of his calling. In all the temptations and provocations of life, he retains control, holds his tongue, and keeps peace in his heart.

Next the apostle speaks of **patience** (Gr. *makrothumia*). The main thought here is refusal to retaliate. We are called to endure through all—insults, foolishness, setbacks, even disasters—and not lash out. The great example of patience given us is the Lord Himself. Though our sins and stupidities are always before Him, yet He still has patience with us, not punishing or rebuking, awaiting our repentance. Thus St. Peter tells us to "count the patience of our Lord as salvation" (2 Pet. 3:15). We are called to imitate Him as best we can, having patience with all.

The apostle also speaks of **bearing with** [Gr. *anexomenos*] **one another in love**. To bear with one another is to ignore errors, sins, slights, and stupidities. It is to look past these surface imperfections and continue to serve the other. The Lord was forbearing, for example, when He overlooked His disciples' faithlessness and inability to heal the epileptic boy (Matt. 17:17). "O faithless generation!" He said, "How long am I to bear with you?" (Gr. *anex-omai umon*). Yet despite His disciples' lack of faith, He continued to "love them to the end" (John 13:1). So are we called to bear with one another, covering the other's imperfections with the love of Christ.

All of these virtues are needed if we are to **keep the unity of the Spirit in the bond of peace**. This **unity** (Gr. *enoteta*) is the unity given by the Spirit, as the Lord's sovereign and unbreakable gift to His Church. Unity is one of the marks or characteristics of the Church: it is One, as well as Holy, Catholic, and Apostolic. This unity is not something we are called upon to produce ourselves. The Church's unity is not manmade. It is not the unity of those in a club or group who have decided to get along. Rather, it is an ontological reality, rooted in the essential being of the Church. The unity that binds us one to another is the very unity that unites the Father to the Son (John 17:20–23), the divine unity that underlies and binds together the universe (see Col. 1:17). The fallen and unredeemed world is characterized by *dis*unity—by wars, factions, quarreling, hatred, and mutual separation. Xenophobia—hatred of foreigners, of those who are different—is our global characteristic. Thus, salvation comes to us as the restoration of unity. As the Kontakion for Pentecost sings, "When the Most High came down and confused the tongues, He divided the nations; but when He distributed the tongues of fire, He called all to unity."

It is this divine unity which is produced in our communities by **the Spirit** and which we are called to be **eager to keep**. We do this by not shaking off **the bond of peace**. Peace of heart within and peace of relations between us binds us together in a mutual **bond**. This bond or shackle is not oppressive, but liberating. For it not only unites us one to another, but unites all to the Lord. By not breaking this bond, thus shattering the peace between us, we preserve the Church's unity and walk worthy of our calling.

ॐ ॐ ॐ ॐ ॐ

ॐ ॐ ॐ ॐ ॐ

4   *For there is* one Body and one Spirit, as also
    you were called in one hope of your calling;
5   one Lord, one Faith, one Baptism,
6   one God and Father of *us* all who is over all
    and through all and in all.

As an encouragement to help them maintain unity among themselves, St. Paul stresses what they share in common. Namely, they
all belong to **one Body** and have all received **one** and the same **Spirit**.
In their local communities, there is a lot of diversity, with many
different kinds of personalities. The Church encompasses all races,
colors, political opinions, and classes. This inevitably makes for tension within the community, as all these different types strive to live
in peace. St. Paul here calls attention to the basic characteristics of
the community and the unity which goes deeper than all their diversity. Beyond all their differences, they are all part of **one Body**
and thus should have the same care that one limb of the human
body has for the others (see his analogy in 1 Cor. 12:14–26). And as
a human body is animated by a human spirit, so it is with the Body
of Christ: all in the Body have received the same **Spirit** in their
baptismal initiation. Thus, all have the same divine Life, the same access to the Father, whatever their different social stations in the world.

Thought of the **one Spirit** leads St. Paul to think of the age to
come, that one and common **hope** to which all were called—for the
sacramental gift of the Holy Spirit is our participation in the powers of the age to come. Whatever their different and varied earthly
circumstances, they are all called to the one Kingdom.

Thought of the heavenly Kingdom leads St. Paul to think of the
Lord enthroned there. He mentions as common **one Lord, one Faith,
one Baptism.** (The cadence and rhythm suggest that he draws here
from some prior hymn or perhaps some catechismal instruction.)
The three are indissolubly linked. There is but **one Lord**—the
one preached by the apostles in their **one Faith**. There were of
course other "Jesuses" and other versions of the Faith circulating

(see 2 Cor. 11:4). Heretical distortions of the apostolic Faith were to be found even then. But these are not the genuine Gospel of the apostles, not the true Faith; these distortions offer but a counterfeit version of the true Lord. It is only in the apostolic Church—held together by each local community holding to the same Faith—that saving and authentic discipleship to the Lord is possible. It is to this community that entrance is made by baptism. It is here called **one Baptism** because, wherever one went in those days, whether to Ephesus, Corinth, Rome, or even to the ends of the earth, one found in the apostolic and catholic churches there the same Faith, and one's baptism was recognized as admitting one to the same Body. It was not the case that, being baptized at Ephesus, one went to Corinth and found there a different Faith, a different Church. The same Church was present there as well, and they recognized another Christian as belonging to the same family as themselves, possessing the same baptism.

Finally St. Paul mentions, as the climax of all they hold in common, the **one God and Father of** *us* **all**. They all share not only membership in the same Body, the same sacramental Gift of the Spirit; not only the same heavenly destination and earthly experience of the Lord in His Church. They all share the same **Father.** He is described as being **over all and through all and in all**. That is, He is the Source of the life of each one and of all the world. He is sovereignly **over all** the world, the great and universal Pantocrator. He is **through all**, working His purposes in all creation. He is **in all**, the inner life of all who live. Since they all share the same life-giving Father, they are truly all brothers. With such things held in common, how can they not strive to walk together in peace?

୫ଡ଼ ୫ଡ଼ ୫ଡ଼ ୫ଡ଼ ୫ଡ଼

7   But grace was given to each one of us accord-
    ing to the measure of Christ's gift.
8   Therefore it says, "Having ascended on high,
    he captured captivity, and gave gifts to men."
9   (Now *this word* "He ascended," *what does it*

> *mean but that* He also had descended into the lower parts of the earth?
>
> 10 He who descended is Himself also He who ascended far above all the heavens, that He might fill all things.)
>
> 11 And He *it was who* gave some *as* apostles, and some prophets, and some evangelists, and some shepherds and teachers,
>
> 12 for the equipping of the saints for the work of service, *and* the building of the Body of Christ;
>
> 13 until we all attain to the unity of the Faith, and of the real-knowledge of the Son of God, to a perfect manhood, to the measure of the stature of the fullness of Christ,

The unity St. Paul stresses does not preclude diversity, just as the human body is all one, but still has diversity of function in its members. Though we are all one, **each one of us** was given his own **grace** (his own task and function in the Body), **measured** out to us as **Christ's gift** according to our capacity to receive it. These spiritual gifts are distributed by the Lord as part of the riches of His ascended glory and His Resurrection bounty to His people.

Here St. Paul explains this with a verse from Ps. 68:18. In its original context, this psalm was about Yahweh's victorious ascent of Mount Zion. As a king returned from battle in triumph and received plunder ("gifts") from his captive enemies to distribute them in turn to his followers, so Yahweh's Ark came in triumph to Mount Zion, where He was to receive tribute from His conquered foes.

St. Paul applies this psalm as referring to Christ. The **ascending**, in this messianic application, refers not just to Yahweh's ascent of Zion. It refers ultimately to Christ's Ascension to heaven, after His earthly struggles, wherein He **captured captivity** and conquered death for our sakes. The **gifts** now refer not just to the plunder and tribute of the nations, received and distributed. They refer ultimately to the spiritual gifts Christ gives to His disciples, the result of His plundering of Satan's usurped authority and of the spiritual riches of His ascended glory.

These gifts are many and varied. Some, for example, are given the gift of being **apostles**, some are gifted to be **prophets**, some **evangelists**, yet others **shepherds and teachers**. The list, of course, is not exhaustive. Rather, it simply illustrates the variety of all the gifts of Christ, who measures out His grace **to each one** in His Body.

In verse 9, St. Paul interrupts his main point by interjecting an explanation about the Ascension to which he has just referred. He points out that this verse of Psalm 68 actually presupposes the Incarnation of Christ. For how, he reasons, could the Most High God **ascend**? How could the Highest *go up*? Go up where? For God already dwells in the heights. To say, he points out, that God could **ascend**, presupposes that He has already **descended**—that He has already taken our flesh and come "down" to us on earth. And not only to earth, but even **into the lower parts of the earth**—to the grave, to death, to Hades, to share the full extremities of our human condition. Only after such a descent and humbling did He then ascend in glory **far above all the heavens**—not to abandon us, but rather **that He might fill all things**. St. Paul could not mention the ascension in Psalm 68 without teaching us, in a kind of excited footnote, how it fits in with the mystery of Christ of which He has been speaking (see 1:20–23).

The apostle continues to elaborate on the **gifts** that Christ gave to His Church. (The **He** in v. 11 is emphatic in the Greek. St. Paul doesn't just say that "He [Jesus] gave His Church these gifts." Rather, "It was *He*, Jesus, who gave His Church these gifts—**He who ascended far above all the heavens**—and no one else.") That is, the spiritual gifts in the Church are the result of His ascended glory, the fruit of His fullness who **fills all things**. Thus, these **gifts** are not arbitrary presents given out by the Lord, as if He might equally well have *not* given gifts to His Church. Rather, they are a part of His glorification in which we are made to share, an intrinsic part of our own *theosis*.

St. Paul mentions the more prominent among His gifts: **apostles** and **prophets** (already mentioned in 2:20 and 3:5), **evangelists**,

shepherds and teachers. As said before, the list is not intended to be exhaustive. It merely illustrates the nature of the Lord's bounty by mentioning some of the higher and more important gifts (see 1 Cor. 12:27–31, where St. Paul mentions "apostles, prophets, and teachers" as the first, second, and third appointments in the Church body).

Evangelists (Gr. *evaggelistes*) are those in a local community who have a gift for communicating and preaching the Good News (Gr. *evaggelizo*). It would include not only preaching to the (as yet) unconverted, but also debating and defending the Faith as apologists. (St. Stephen did this evangelical work when he disputed with the synagogue, speaking with a wisdom and persuasiveness they could not withstand [Acts 7:9, 10].) St. Philip the Deacon (feast day October 11) was an evangelist (Acts 21:8). St. Timothy was urged by St. Paul to "do the work of an evangelist," preaching the word in season and out of season (2 Tim. 4:2, 5). An evangelist differed from an apostle in that an apostle traveled widely with the fullness of authority in the Church, whereas evangelist seems to have been a stationary calling. They were prominent as those who converted many and helped the local church to grow.

Shepherds and teachers were two distinct offices, whose functions sometimes greatly overlapped. The term **shepherd** (Gr. *poimen*) was originally a political term, a nation's shepherd being its ruler or king (see, e.g., Ezek. 34:1–10). The term was applied to the rulers of the Church, not only because they ruled the Church (see 1 Tim. 5:17, "presbyters who rule") but also because they were to have the same solicitous care for the Church that the shepherd had for his flock (see 1 Pet. 5:2). These presbyters or shepherds were sometimes distinguished from the related office of teacher. There were teachers at Antioch (Acts 13:1) along with the prophets. That the term *teacher* is not simply a synonym for shepherd or presbyter is apparent from 1 Timothy 5:17. There it says that the shepherd-presbyters were to be considered worthy of double honor, "especially those who labor in preaching and teaching." This tells us that not all presbyters preached and taught, so that those who did were considered worthy of "double honor." It was specifically the function of the teachers to teach, though presbyters might do this as well. St. Paul here groups them together as one category (both nouns are governed by the one Greek particle *tous de*) because their function so often coincided. It is a reference to what we would call the local clergy, the teaching presbyters of the Church.

St. Paul says that these ministries were given **for the equipping of the saints for the work of service,** *and* **the building of the Body of Christ**. The original Greek indicates that the thought is *not* that the gifts of these offices are given (1) for the equipping of the saints, (2) for the work of service, and (3) for the building of the Body (i.e. for three different ends, all done by the clergy). The Greek is clear that the thought is rather that these clerical gifts were given to equip the saints so that *they*, the saints, could perform (1) the work of service and (2) the building of the Body.

This is an important distinction, for it means that it is the *saints,* all the faithful laity, who perform this work of service and upbuilding—not just the clergy. The job of the clergy is to *equip the saints* to do this work, not to do the work instead themselves.

This entire mention of these offices in the Church (offices of apostle, prophet, evangelist, shepherd, and teacher) occurs within the more general discussion of walking worthy of our calling and of preserving unity in the Body (vv. 1–3). St. Paul does not mention them in order to compose a blueprint or handbook for Church order. Rather, he is exhorting all to maturity and holiness. His thought is that, within the context of unity (vv. 4–6), diverse gifts of grace are given within the Body (vv. 7–11), and that all these gifts are given for no other purpose than to serve the common good— **until we all attain to the unity of the Faith**. It is similar to what he writes in 1 Cor. 12:1–12. The spiritual gifts we have, the individual diversity with which we have been gifted, are given to us so that we may use them to "strive to build up the Church" (1 Cor. 12:12) and to serve our neighbor. All the gifts—even the most important and prominent ones of apostle, prophet, evangelist, shepherd, and teacher—are given only for this purpose. So it is that they all must use their individual callings and gifts not to glorify themselves and to think their task more important than their brother's. How easy it is to fight and quarrel, feeling our gifts and position entitle us to special treatment and extra respect! Against such temptations, St. Paul encourages us to use all our gifts in the service of others in the Body.

The ministries are to be used for **the equipping of the saints**. The word for **equipping** is the Greek word *katartismos*, meaning "to put into proper condition." It is used elsewhere to mean "to mend" (as when the disciples were mending their nets, Mark 1:19), and to mean "to complete the lack" (as when St. Paul wanted to teach and fill up the lack in the church's faith, 1 Thess. 3:10). Thus here St. Paul says that all the gifts and offices in the Church have as their purpose providing the faithful with all that they need to do their job. And what is the job of the faithful, of the holy laity? To do the **work of service** [Gr. *diakonia*] *and* **the building of the Body of Christ**. The faithful, taught and empowered by their clergy, are to serve one another, even as their Lord girded Himself with a servant's towel and served them (John 13:1–17), and thus to begin to heal the world. This spiritual growth is described as the **building** [Gr. *oikodome*] **of the Body of Christ** (see Eph. 2:22). It is only as we serve one another that true growth in the Body is possible and the Church is built.

This equipping of the saints to do their holy work of building the Church is to go on until our final goal is reached—that of true spiritual maturity. This maturity is described as **unity** with one another in the Faith. The sign of maturity in a community is their unity, their walking with one another in peace and love (see Eph. 4:3; Col. 3:14). Since the Church's unity is itself the unity of the Godhead (such as the Father has with the Son, see John 17:20–23), our full maturity in God necessarily involves our unity with one another. Thus, if we have no peace with our Christian brethren, we have no true peace with God, and any perceived peace we have with Him is then an illusion.

This maturity is also described as attaining to **the real-knowledge** [Gr. *epignosis*] **of the Son of God**. As mentioned above, the term *epignosis* is distinguished from mere *gnosis* in being a greater, more intimate knowledge. As matured believers, we do not just know *about* the Son of God—we know Him personally. Our life consists of a relationship with Him in which we know, by experience, what kind of a God we serve. We ourselves can testify, in the words of the Great Prokeimenon, "Who is so great a God as our God? You are the God who does wonders!"

This maturity is further described as our attaining to **perfect** [or mature] **manhood** (Gr. *andra teleion*). The word for *man* (Gr. *aner*, "male, adult") is different from that used in Eph. 2:25 (Gr. *anthropos*, "human being"). Here it refers to our spiritual coming of age, so that we are no longer spiritually childish, concerned only with ourselves and our toys. As St. Paul says elsewhere, "When I became a man [Gr. *aner*], I put away childish things" (1 Cor. 13:11).

Finally, this maturity is described as attaining to **the measure of the stature of the fullness of Christ**. The **stature** to which we are to attain is nothing less than that of the **fullness of Christ** (see Eph. 3:19). It is His **perfect manhood** into which we shall grow; when we are fully grown, we shall be like Him, our Teacher (see Luke 6:40), entirely conformed to His image (Rom. 8:29).

---

୫ ୫ ୫ ୫ ୫

14 that we no longer should be infants, wave-tossed and carried about by every wind of teaching, by the trickery of men, by craftiness in the scheming of deception;

15 but truthing it in love, we are to grow up in all *things* into Him who is the Head, *into* Christ,

16 from whom the whole Body, being co-joined and knit-together by every supplying joint, according to the measured working of each one part, makes the Body grow for the building of itself in love.

As we reach spiritual maturity, we are no longer vulnerable and at risk, as immature children are, being gullible and easily deceived. For there have always been in the world religious opportunists, spiritual shysters, promoters of passing fashions and fads. The immature were easily taken in by these, helpless as a **wave-tossed** ship in a storm before every blowing **wind of teaching** from these men. These men were the initiators of religious "movements" (advertised by them as the latest and most up-to-date of the works of God). St. Paul recognizes their work as mere **trickery** (Gr. *kubeia*). This word is used to mean literally "dice-rolling" and, by association, "cheating." He denounces their religious persuasiveness as **craftiness in the scheming of deception**. The word for *scheming* (Gr. *methodeia*) means "ruses, stratagems." St. Paul would have us know that, though such teachers promise enlightenment and deeper truth, all their fancy rhetoric is simply a scam, a smooth con job for passing off **deception**. Our spiritual maturity gives us an immunity to such men and to the fads they promote.

As an alternative to entanglement in such error, we are to grow closer to the Lord. This is done as we **truth it in love**. The verb coined here as **to truth** is an attempt to translate the Greek verb *aletheuo*, meaning to deal truthfully and truly, to both say and do the truth (Gr. *aletheia*). (No single English word is entirely adequate as a translation.) St. Paul says here that in all our dealings with one another, we are to manifest the truth. We are to renounce half-lies and dubious moral compromises, refusing to use one another for our own selfish ends. We are to respect the dignity of our brothers and deal with them truly, uprightly, in love, without patronizing them. Only so can we **grow up in all** *things,* in every way, into our **Head,** *into* **Christ**. Maturity involves a closer union with our **Head,** the Source of our life. If we hold fast to Him (see Col. 2:19), not being separated by the wiles of heretics, we mature in every way.

Then follows an intricate image—that of a body being given life and health by its head. What Christ supplies, which **makes the Body grow** so that it grows **in love**, is supplied by the proper working of the **joints**. These **joints** are the relationships in the Body of Christ. The Body is **co-joined** (Gr. *sunarmologeo*) and **knit-together** (Gr. *sumbibazo*). Once again, the Greek prefix *sun-* indicates a joint, corporate aspect to Church life. We all together, through our relationships one with another, give form to the Body, and supply it with what it needs to move and grow. We each make our own contribution to the whole through our relationships and mutual service. Whether by exalted service (such as that of apostles or prophets) or less prominent forms of ministry, we all contribute to the overall functioning of the Body, so that it **builds itself in love.**

§VI.2   Maturity of putting on love (4:17—5:2)

ॐ ॐ ॐ ॐ ॐ

17 This therefore I speak, and witness in *the* Lord, that you *yourselves* walk no longer as the Gentiles also walk, in the uselessness of their mind,

18 being darkened in their understanding, estranged from the life of God because of the ignorance that is in them, because of the hardness of their heart;

19 and they, having cast off all feeling, have delivered themselves to sensuality for the working of all uncleanness with greediness.

St. Paul here begins afresh his exhortation to mature in the Lord. As he began by invoking his moral authority as "the prisoner of the Lord" (4:1), so here too he summons all the authority he can muster. **I speak, and witness** [Gr. *martyromai*] **in** *the* **Lord**, he says— that is, he gives his solemn word before the Lord, calling Him as witness (Gr. *martyr*, see Rom. 1:9; 2 Cor. 1:23). He gives as much weight as he can to his exhortation to them to **walk** and live differently than **the Gentiles** do. (Note that he speaks of **the Gentiles** as if these were a different group from his hearers. For the Ephesian Christians may have been Gentiles once, but now they are not. They no longer belong to the Gentile world, but to the Kingdom.)

The Gentiles are described as walking **in the uselessness of their mind.** That is, their minds are filled with empty, useless vanities, trite things and trifles, complete time-wasters. Their thoughts are

darkened; no beam of light or life from God penetrates their minds; they are entirely **estranged** from the divine life because of their **ignorance** and their **hardness of heart**. Note: it is not that God rejects them and refuses them light and life. Rather, their **ignorance** and **hardness of heart** repel and keep God's life away. Their life choices deny God access; they do not know Him because they refuse to know Him. They are willfully ignorant of Him, having hardened their heart against His love and life. They have **cast off all feeling** (Gr. *apelgekotes*, indicating an insensitivity to pain or any stimulus, an inability to feel any sensation).

Having become thus deadened, they seek to feel alive by plunging into **sensuality**. This **sensuality** (Gr. *aselgeia*) is not merely indulgence in sexual, fleshly desires. It has been described as impudence, the kind of debauched and open, flagrant sin which does not even try to hide. They abandon themselves to this **sensuality**, working **all uncleanness with greediness**. That is, they stuff themselves full of every kind of filthiness and perversion. The word *greediness* (Gr. *pleonexia*) indicates "craving," addiction, being consumed with desire. The thought is one of frantic pursuit of every available sinful experience. The Gentiles, St. Paul says, underneath their air of sophistication and urbanity, are like the walking dead. They can no longer feel anything, and in their desperation to experience sensation, they frantically try every extreme and forbidden pleasure, like men who stab themselves with knives in order to feel something and assure themselves they are still alive. It is this nightmare world which St. Paul tells his hearers to have done with.

ॐ ॐ ॐ ॐ ॐ

20 But you *yourselves* did not thus learn Christ
21 (if indeed you have heard Him and have been taught in Him, as truth is in Jesus).
22 Put off the old man, which concerns your former conduct, which is being corrupted, according to the desires of deceit,
23 *and* be renewed in the spirit of your mind,

> **24 and put on the new man, which has been created according to God in righteousness and holiness of the truth.**

St. Paul refers here to their original baptismal catechesis. The phrase **learn Christ** indicates the original lessons of their discipleship as catechumens. The verb *to learn* (Gr. *manthano*) is cognate with the word for "disciple" (Gr. *mathetes*) and in fact means "to become a disciple" or pupil. It is the fulfillment of the Lord's commission to His Church, "Make disciples [Gr. *matheteuo*] of all nations, baptizing them in the Name of the Father and of the Son and of the Holy Spirit, teaching them to observe all I commanded you" (Matt. 28:19). When the Ephesians then first became disciples, sealing their catechismal lessons in Holy Baptism, they learned a different way of life from their former Gentile life—**if indeed** they heard the Gospel and were taught the truth at all! In saying **if indeed** they were taught, St. Paul does not express doubt that they were. Rather, he says that since they obviously *had* heard and been taught the truth, they must have heard this before when they first became disciples. There is no excuse then not to live it!

The teaching they were given as catechumens was consistent with the **truth in Jesus**. That is, in Jesus, **the truth** was fully manifested at last. By "truth," St. Paul means not a set of propositions and statements (which could be true or false). He means truth in the Hebraic sense: truth as soundness, bedrock reality, sanity, light. With the coming of Jesus, light has shone in the darkness of the world and we can see ourselves as we really are. The life and words of the Lord Jesus reveal the way in which we should go.

This, St. Paul says, is what they learned as disciples of Christ— that they **put off** their **old** (Gr. *palaios*, "old, earlier") self and **put on** their **new** (Gr. *kainos*, "brand-new, fresh") self, the new creation. The image of putting off and putting on is taken from their baptismal experience and expresses its meaning. At their baptism, they put off their old garments (as a preparation for their triple immersion) and then, after their baptism, put on garments again. This action becomes a metaphor for what was accomplished in their baptism itself, namely, the complete putting off and renunciation of their old life and their putting on and assuming of their new one. (The verbs are both in the aorist tense, indicating a once-and-for-all completed action. This indicates that the work of putting off and putting on has already been accomplished at their baptism. It remains, however, for them to apply it and work it in their life. They are called to "become what they are.")

St. Paul compares the old life with the new one. The old life they **put off** is **being corrupted, according to the desires of deceit**. These old **desires** (Gr. *epithumia*; see Eph. 2:3) are called here deceitful because they promise lasting joy and satisfaction but ultimately disappoint. Indulgence in such *desires* does not bring about the advertised fulfillment. Rather, it results in corruption and death.

As the alternative, we have **put on the new man** and been made a part of the New Creation. Unlike this present old fallen creation, this has been created **according to God**, with all His uprightness, life, and joy. It is made in **righteousness and holiness of the truth**. Here there is no place for deceit or unfulfilled promises. In living in the new creation of **righteousness and holiness**, we are assured of the promised eternal joy. Our task now is to **be renewed** [Gr. *ananeoo*] **in the spirit of your mind**. Unlike the verbal forms for our **putting off** and **putting on** (the aorist, past tense), this verb is in the present tense. It means that this renewal is a present and continuing process, an ongoing work. Our inner attitudes and motivations (**spirit**, see Rom. 1:9) must be transformed by our constant attentive striving. The result is that we are made new and young (Gr. *neos*, "young"). We are not to let the Gentile world age us, making us bitter and cynical. In Christ, we are **renewed**, and our youthful vigor is restored.

ॐ ॐ ॐ ॐ ॐ

25 Therefore, put off falsehood; speak truth, each
   one with his neighbor, for we are members one
   of another.

26 Be angry, and do not sin; do not let the sun
go down on your provocation,
27 and do not give a place to the devil.
28 The thief must thieve no longer; but rather let
him toil, working what is good with his hands,
so that he will have *something* to impart to one
who has need.
29 Let no corrupt word proceed from your
mouth, but only such as is good for building
up according to the *present* need, that it may
give grace to those who hear.
30 And do not grieve the Holy Spirit of God, in
whom you were sealed for the day of redemption.

We are to be renewed in our inner attitudes, just as we put on
the new creation at our baptism. What does this mean specifically?
What does this constant striving for inner renewal mean?

St. Paul answers this in beginning this section by saying **Therefore**. Here he begins to spell out what this inner renewal means in
terms of our actual behavior. Part of the old man which we **put off**
in baptism was **falsehood**, lying, the whole way of life which considers that getting what we want is more important than telling the
truth. Instead of this, we are to **speak truth** to each other. (Here he
quotes from Zech. 8:16, where God instructs us to "speak the truth
to one another, not to devise evil in your hearts and make no false
oath," for these things He hates.)

St. Paul gives the further reason that we should thus love one
another and speak the truth because **we are members one of
another**. As one member of the physical body cares for the other
members, since all are interconnected, so we believers should have
such care for one another. The good of our neighbor in Christ is
our own good. We may **be angry**, but we should **not sin**. Once
again, St. Paul here quotes Psalm 4:4 (in the LXX version). There
we are)exhorted to "feel compunction on our beds for what is said
in our hearts." That is, when we lie down at night, we are to let go

of our anger, so that the setting sun does not find us still unforgiving. For it is this unforgiveness, this refusal to let go of a grudge, this nursing of anger and resentment, that **gives a place** and opportunity **to the devil.**

This life of renewal is very practical. We are not to lie to one another, using each other. We are not to hold grudges. The one who formerly stole must **thieve no longer.** Thievery, with its roots in prideful laziness, which would rather steal than work, must give way and be replaced with its positive counter-virtue. So far from taking what belongs to others, the former shoplifter and con man must now **toil, working what is good with his hands** so that he may give what belongs to him to others **who have need.** The negative taking is replaced with the positive giving as the thief becomes the almsgiver.

St. Paul also says to **let no corrupt** [Gr. *sapros*, "foul, putrid"] **word proceed from your mouth.** As the Lord said, we must give an account for every idle word we utter (Matt. 12:36). We must then "set a guard over our mouth and keep watch over the door of our lips" (Ps. 141:3). The sentries of our inner attention must not let any words pass through which are **corrupt.**

Rather, our words should be **good for building up,** for edifying our brethren, suited to the **need** of each moment, so that those who hear them will receive **grace** (Gr. *charis*). The word **grace** here is probably used to mean, not God's grace (as in Eph. 2:5), but rather "benefit" from us. St. Paul uses the word with this meaning in 2 Corinthians 1:15, where he says he intended to visit the Corinthians twice so that they might have a "double grace"—that is, twice the benefit.

As a further incentive to renewal, St. Paul says to **not grieve the Holy Spirit.** (It is apparent that this exhortation should be read as summing up the former verses [25–29] rather than as introducing the next verses [31f], since it begins **And do not grieve**—this **and** connecting it to the preceding verses.) This is a powerful incentive. We should speak the truth, forgive each other, giving alms instead of stealing, speaking only beneficial words, because to refuse to love one another would **grieve the Holy Spirit of God.** To walk in the old ways of the Gentiles would be to risk the departure of the Holy Spirit from our lives. In our baptism, we were **sealed** in Him until the Second Coming, when our **redemption** would be complete (see Eph. 1:13, 14). How tragic it would be to grieve and lose Him who was to be our guarantee of final salvation!

ॐ ॐ ॐ ॐ ॐ

31 Let all bitterness and indignation and wrath and clamor and reviling be removed from you, with all malice.

32 Be kind to one another, tenderhearted, forgiving one another, as God in Christ also forgave you.

5 1 Therefore be imitators of God, as beloved children;

2 and walk in love, just as Christ also loved you and delivered up Himself for us, an offering and a sacrifice to God, an odor of fragrance.

St. Paul continues with his exhortation to put off the old man. We are to renounce and remove from our lives all kinds of anger, for "the anger of man does not work the righteousness of God" (James 1:20). Specifically, St. Paul mentions **bitterness** (Gr. *pikria*), which is longstanding resentment, the brooding grudges we cherish and guard as if they were hidden treasure. He also mentions **indignation** (Gr. *thumos*), which is an explosion of temper, a sudden outbreak of fury. Also to be renounced is **wrath** (Gr. *orge*), which is habitual anger, the frightful disposition of someone always mad at something. St. Paul also forbids **clamor** (Gr. *krauge*), which is shouting and yelling. **Reviling** (Gr. *blasphemia*) is forbidden, meaning not just the cool backbiting of gossip, but more specifically here the angry tossing of insults and verbal abuse. Finally, he mentions as forbidden **all malice** (Gr. *kakia*), which is all kinds of bad feeling, ill will, and readiness to think the worst of someone.

All these kinds of anger are to be removed from our lives. In its place, we are to put the positive virtues. We are to speak and act with **kind**ness (Gr. *chrestos*), caring for one another, looking for ways to help. We are to be **tenderhearted** (Gr. *eusplagchnos*), having compassion, so that our heart goes out to the other person. Whenever there is a sin against us (as there inevitably will be when we live in community), we respond by **forgiving one another**, even as we were ourselves forgiven by God.

In this way, we will be **imitators of God**, bearing the family likeness that **beloved children** do to their Father. For God forgives us in Christ, and as His own children, we also forgive one another and **walk in love**. Once again, the work of the Lord provides us with our paradigm and pattern. We love because the Lord **loved** us (Gr. *agapesen*, aorist, once-for-all past tense) and **delivered Himself up for us** on the Cross. This Sacrifice was an **odor of fragrance**— i.e. it was acceptable to God. What St. Paul implies here is that, as Christ loved us and sacrificed Himself for us, so our lives will be an acceptable sacrifice to God if we also love one another. As St. John says, "He laid down His life for us and we ought to lay down our lives for the brethren" (1 John 3:16). All of this is the life St. Paul commends to us, solemnly urging it upon us as "worthy of our calling" (4:1).

§VI.3 Maturity of shunning darkness for light (5:3–21)

༄ ༄ ༄ ༄ ༄

3 But fornication or any uncleanness or greed must not even be named among you, as is proper among saints;

4 and there must be no filthiness and foolish-talking, or jesting, which are not fitting, but rather thanksgiving.

5 For you know *and* understand this, that no fornicator or unclean or greedy *person* (who is an idolater) has an inheritance in the Kingdom of Christ and God.

> 6 Let no one deceive you with empty words, for
> because of these things the wrath of God comes
> upon the sons of disobedience.

Fornication . . . must not even be named among you: St. Paul continues to exhort them to walk in a manner worthy of their calling, telling them to shun the darkness, fleeing from it to such an extent that certain sins are **not even named** among them. That is, they are to conduct themselves **as is proper among saints** so that the world around them will not even accuse them of such things and there will not even be the rumor of them happening in their midst.

Prominent in the Gentile darkness that they are to shun is sexual sin. Indeed, **fornication** (Gr. *porneia*) was not considered a sin at all (for men at least!), and in that sex-soaked society it was taken for granted. Thus it is that the apostolic Church had to make a special point of forbidding it to their recent Gentile converts (e.g. Acts 15:29; 1 Cor. 6:12–20; 1 Thess. 4:3). As such, it heads here the list of sins. Along with **fornication**, St. Paul tells them to flee from **any uncleanness** (Gr. *akatharsia*), meaning any form of sexual sin (such as, for example, pornography).

Also banned is **greed** (Gr. *pleonexia*, see its use in 4:19). It is equated with **idolatry**, since the person consumed with desire for material things has made Mammon into his God. As the Lord warned us, we cannot serve both God and Mammon (Matt. 6:24). Christians are to aim at simplicity of living (see our Lord's counsel to sell our possessions, Luke 12:33) and those who insatiably crave more and more "cannot enter the Kingdom of Heaven" (Matt. 19:23). They have made perishable things their true god and will perish with them.

St. Paul considers these sins to be entirely lethal and of the utmost danger to our lives in Christ. There were some who suggested that Holy Baptism was enough and that it was sufficient to become Christians and simply start on the path to final salvation. It did not matter ultimately how one lived, as long as one had made a commitment to Christ. St. Paul denounces these as **empty words** and warns his hearers not to be deceived by them. It is because of precisely these sins that **the wrath of God** will come upon those **sons of disobedience** who commit them. In fact, he says that his hearers have already learned (from their catechismal instruction, no doubt; see 4:20) that no one whose life is characterized by fornication, uncleanness, or greed **has an inheritance in the Kingdom of Christ and God.**

As well as the deadly sins of fornication, uncleanness, and greed, St. Paul also warns them against other sins, for these sins are the "thin edge of the wedge" to the greater ones. They must watch their words, for words are powerful, affecting and changing both ourselves and those around us. The guarding of our language is the first and important step to guarding the rest of our behavior (see James 3:3–5). Thus St. Paul writes that there must be no **filthiness** or baseness (Gr. *aischrotes*), no **foolish-talking** (Gr. *morologia*), and no **jesting** (Gr. *eutrapelia*). In saying this, he does not forbid all humor, laughter, or lightness of heart. A sense of humor is a divine gift and is found in many (some would say in all) holy people. What St. Paul here forbids is irreverent, blasphemous humor, the uncontrolled spirit that ridicules everything and holds nothing sacred, that oversteps all bounds with profanity and what is sometimes called "inappropriate humor." All of this talk should be far from lips that praise God and receive the Holy Eucharist. In its place, our talk should be full of **thanksgiving** (Gr. *eucharistia*). Instead of seeing the world as mere material for obscene satire, we should experience it as the gift of God, and "give thanks in all circumstances" (1 Thess. 5:18).

꒰ꔹ꒱ ꒰ꔹ꒱ ꒰ꔹ꒱ ꒰ꔹ꒱ ꒰ꔹ꒱

7   Therefore do not be co-partakers with them;
8   for you were once darkness, but now you are light in the Lord; walk as children of light
9   (for the fruit of the light *is* in all goodness and righteousness and truth),
10 proving what is well-pleasing to the Lord.

> 11 Do not co-share in the unfruitful works of
>   darkness, but rather even expose them;
> 12 for it is shameful even to speak of the things
>   they do in secret.
> 13 But all things exposed by the light become
>   visible, for anything that becomes visible is light.
> 14 Therefore it says, "Awake, sleeper, and arise
>   from the dead, and Christ will shine on you."

Because "the wrath of God" will come upon "the sons of disobedience" (v. 6) who live in these sins, we are urged **not** to **be
co-partakers with them**, lest God's wrath fall upon us too. **Once** we
also were such sons of disobedience and were **darkness**. Now, however, having been illumined in Holy Baptism, we are **light** (Gr. *phos*)
because Christ has **shone** (Gr. *epiphausko*) on us (vv. 13, 14). Quoting a Christian hymn (which was based on Isaiah 60:1), St. Paul
describes our baptism as our having been raised **from the dead** by
Christ, our **awaking** like a **sleeper** from the sleep of sin and death.
Christ the Light now **shines** on us in our new life, making us
children of light. (It is for this reason that baptism is called "illumination"; see Heb. 6:4.) In this new life, we bear the **fruit of the
light**—that is, deeds reflecting **all goodness, righteousness and
truth**. Instead of **the unfruitful works of darkness** (deeds that bear
no life-giving fruit, coming from lives that are of no use to others),
we bear the fruit of a changed life so that others derive from us
benefit and blessing. Thus we **prove**, or learn by the experience of
doing, **what is well-pleasing to the Lord**.

The change is complete and total, light being the absolute
opposite of darkness. Therefore, now that Christ the Light **shines**
on us, making us **light in the Lord**, we must live in active opposition to the darkness that surrounds us. Not only are we not to
co-share in their sins, their **unfruitful works of darkness**, we should
rather even expose them, just as light exposes darkness. This is the
true and full meaning of our baptismal illumination, of Christ shining upon us. As darkness gives place to light (for **anything that
becomes visible is light**), so we are to reprove sin and persuade

127

those in the darkness to join us in **arising from the dead** and shining with the Light of Christ.

ॐ ॐ ॐ ॐ ॐ

15 Therefore beware how strictly you walk, not as unwise but as wise,

16 redeeming the time, because the days are evil.

17 So do not be foolish, but have insight into what the will of the Lord *is*.

18 And do not get drunk with wine, in which is dissipation, but be filled with *the* Spirit,

19 speaking to one another in psalms and hymns and spiritual songs, hymning and singing with your hearts to the Lord;

20 giving thanks always, for all *things*, in *the* Name of our Lord Jesus Christ to God, *who is* also *our* Father;

21 and submit to one another in the fear of Christ.

Because of the eternal incompatibility and strife between darkness and light, **therefore** they must **beware how strictly** (Gr. *akribos*) they **walk**. In saying this, St. Paul does not mean to urge us to a stern and rigorous Pharisaism, a legalistic strictness which would cut ourselves (and others!) no slack. This kind of strictness too easily degenerates into judgmentalism. Rather, he simply warns us to pay attention to our lives, not to be heedless and **unwise** but to take stock of how we are doing. It is too easy to coast along, gradually drifting away from our commitment to the Lord, slowly being hardened by the deceitfulness of sin (Heb. 3:12, 13). We are urged here to regular examination of conscience and to keep our wits about us as we walk through the world, **because the days are evil**. That is, this age is full of temptation and difficulties and it hurries towards its final catastrophe. Therefore, as **wise** men, we are to **redeem the time**, buying up and using every opportunity to do good, doing **the will of the Lord**.

A prominent characteristic of those **evil** days was drunkenness. Along with fornication, it was deeply ingrained in the Gentile culture of that day (as in our own!). Thus St. Paul singles it out for censure. It is **dissipation** (Gr. *asotia*)—that is, recklessness, incorrigibility. The thought is of one lost beyond hope of saving. To immerse oneself in that drunken world is to have broken all bonds and to have given up on God.

As always, St. Paul provides a positive alternative. A man must be filled with something. But rather than being filled with wine, one should be **filled with *the* Spirit**. The verb *be filled* (Gr. *plerousthe*) is in the present tense, meaning that one should be *continually* filled with the Spirit. By penitently persevering in prayer and the sacramental Mysteries of the Church, one continually receives the inflow of the Spirit. This is expressed in **speaking to one another in psalms and hymns and spiritual songs**. (Note the corporate aspect to this life of the Spirit: it is lived in community, so that we speak **to one another**. We need each other to live in the Spirit's fullness.)

The praise which we speak to one another is described as **psalms** (Gr. *psalmois*—the OT Psalter), **hymns** (Gr. *umnois*—fresh musical compositions made by the Church, such as are alluded to in v. 14), and **spiritual songs** (Gr. *odais pneumatikais*—singing in a prophecy, 1 Cor. 14:15). With all of these we sing **with our hearts** to the Lord.

In saying that we sing **with our hearts**, St. Paul does not of course mean that we do not also sing with our voices! Rather, St. Paul urges that our vocal praise come from deep within and that our sung words be the overflow of the heart. As St. John Chrysostom says concerning this passage, "It means paying attention while you are singing. It means not letting your mind drift."

Our song in church is the liturgical expression of what should characterize our whole life. Not only while at church services, but **always** we are to **give thanks** [Gr. *eucharisto*] **for all *things***. The sacramental Eucharist in Church sets the tone for and begins a life of thanksgiving. We are to make our entire life a eucharistic offering to God **in *the* Name of our Lord Jesus Christ**. That is, we are to live as His disciples, doing nothing in our own name, but in everything seeking to act as His ambassadors. Our consecration to Him colors all we do, and changes all our relationships. In our life together, we **submit to one another**, as members of one Body, **in the fear of Christ**. That is, in all our doings with one another, we remember that we belong to Him. Because we respect and reverence the Lord, therefore we have respect and reverence for one another as well.

§VI.4 Maturity of living together in family (5:22—6:9)

22 Wives, *submit* to your own husbands, as to the Lord.

23 For the husband is the head of the wife, as Christ is also the Head of the Church, *He* Himself being the Savior of the Body.

24 But as the Church submits to Christ, thus also the wives ought to *submit* to the husbands in everything.

25 Husbands, love the wives, as Christ also loved the Church and delivered up Himself for her,

26 that He might sanctify her, having cleansed *her* by the washing of the water in *the* Word,

27 that He might present to Himself the Church *as* glorious, not having stain or wrinkle or any such thing; but that she would be holy and blameless.

28 Thus the husbands ought also to love their own wives as their own bodies. He who loves his own wife loves himself;

29 for no one ever hated his own flesh, but nurtures and cherishes it, as Christ also *does* the Church,

30 for we are members of His Body.

31 For this reason "a man will leave his father and mother and shall be joined to his wife

> and the two shall become one flesh."
> 32 This mystery is great; but I am speaking *with regard* to Christ and the Church.
> 33 Nevertheless, you *yourselves* also, each and every one, *is* thus to love his own wife as himself, and the wife *is to* fear her husband.

St. Paul mentioned how our relationship with the Lord changes and colors all our relationships with one another. He now begins to detail how this works, talking about wives and husbands, children and fathers, slaves and their masters.

St. Paul's discussion of the relationship between husbands and wives is governed by his understanding of marriage as a great **mystery** (Gr. *musterion*). That is, the original union of Adam with Eve (which is the beginning and fount of all marriage) contains a significance not originally seen. A *musterion*, we recall, is something whose meaning was long hidden but is now revealed to the initiated (see Eph. 1:9; 3:3f).

What was not seen until now is how marriage points to and finds its fulfillment in **Christ and the Church** (v. 32). To the initiated Christians, we see how the intimate union of husband and wife, the reality of their being **one flesh** and one organism, prophesies the new reality of the Church being one flesh and one Body with Christ. The two realities of husband–wife and Christ–Church are related as type and antitype, as prophecy and fulfillment. Indeed, there is a kind of mutuality and interchangeability in these two realities, and it is difficult to say which is the type and which is the antitype. For one might say that the divine love for mankind is the original and our human, married love is the derivation; that the love of Christ for His Church is the original and that marriage is the pale reflection of this. What is certain is that there is a one-to-one correspondence between the two, so that the relations between husbands and wives should reflect the love of Christ and His Church.

Thus, wives must *submit* to their **husbands as the Church submits to Christ**. As Christ is the **Head** and **Savior** of His Body, the Church, so **the husband is the head of the wife**. Husbands must

131

love their wives as Christ also loved the Church and died for her. And as the Church is Christ's Body, so in a sense the wife is one body with her husband, for, St. Paul says, quoting Genesis 2:24, "the two shall become one flesh." Thus the husband must love his wife as he loves his own body, nurturing and cherishing her. Christ does this with His Body, the Church, and so the husband must do the same with his "body," his wife. This should be no difficult thing, St. Paul says, for no one ever hated his own flesh!

There is no doubt that it is a challenging thing to live out such a great mystery. No wonder Holy Matrimony is counted one of the sacramental Mysteries of the Church! And that the liturgical crowns with which the bride and groom are crowned in the wedding service are considered crowns of martyrdom as well as crowns of glory and honor! But what does it actually mean to try to live out this mystery in daily married life?

In St. Paul's summary of his teaching here in verse 33, the wife is called to fear (Gr. *phobeo*) her husband—that is, to respect him and submit to him. It is all too easy to interpret this submission as the degrading, cringing submission given to a tyrant. Indeed, in the world, where authority is so often misused, submission is all too often a degrading thing forced upon the vanquished. But in the Kingdom, authority is something different—it is a form of service. The Lord has forbidden us this other, worldly type of authority and submission. He said, "You know that rulers of the Gentiles lord it over them and their great men exercise authority over them. It shall not be so among you; but whoever would be great among you must be your servant" (Matt. 20:25, 26). Again, on the night on which He was betrayed, He laid aside His garments, girded Himself with a towel and knelt down to wash His disciples' feet, as a lasting lesson for them. He said, "If I then, your Lord and Teacher, have washed your feet, you also ought to wash one another's feet. For I have given you an example" (John 13:14, 15). In all this, He showed us that in the Church, authority is given to serve and submission is the glad and voluntary acceptance of this service. Submission does not involve a loss of dignity nor imply any essential inequality—for Christ submits to the Father, His Head, even though He is eternally co-equal with the Father and one in essence with Him (1 Cor. 11:3; 15:28). The wife is therefore called to **submit** to her husband in that she follows his godly lead, accepting his service, responsibility, and spiritual oversight for herself and the family.

The husband is called to **love his own wife as himself** (v. 33). That is, he is to serve her as Christ serves the Church (see John 13:1–17, mentioned above). Like the task of the wife, the husband's role is very challenging. As Christ **delivered up Himself** and died for His Bride, to be **the Savior of the Body**, so the husband must "die" for his wife, crucifying his own will and desires in order to serve her.

For Christ gives him the pattern and paradigm. He died on the Cross to **sanctify** the Church, having **cleansed** us in Holy Baptism by **the washing of the water** and *the* **Word** of the Gospel, applied through the baptismal invocation of the Holy Trinity. This **sanctified** us (see John 17:17–19), setting us apart from the world as His own Bride, so that on the Last Day He might present to Himself the Church in all glory—having no **stain or wrinkle**, but entirely **holy and blameless** (see 1:4). Behold the love of Christ for His Bride!—He does all things necessary for her eternal joy and salvation. He truly is **the Savior of the Body**, dying for the glory of His Beloved. This is the pattern and example given to the husband—to love his wife like this, as **Christ loved the Church.**

ॐॐ ॐ ॐ ॐ ॐ

6 1 **Children, obey your parents in the Lord, for this is righteous.**

2 **"Honor your father and mother" (which is *the* first commandment with a promise),**

3 **so that it may be well with you and that you may live long on the earth.**

4 **Fathers, do not anger your children, but nurture them in the discipline and admonition of the Lord.**

The relationship of children to parents is dealt with next, the **fathers** taking the main responsibility for discipline, in accord with the cultural norms of that day.

The children are to **obey** their parents **in the Lord**—that is, as a part of their discipleship to Christ. (It is assumed in this that the **children** here are minors living in dependence upon their parents, for the **fathers** are next exhorted to **nurture them** in the instruction of the Lord. That is, it is assumed that the task of raising young children and forming their characters is still ongoing. After the children are adults, it is too late for the fathers to **nurture them** or bring them up any more!) This obedience, St. Paul says, is **righteous** (Gr. *dikaios*)—that is, being pleasing to God, it brings His blessing. (Compare 2 Cor. 9:9 for the use of the word "righteousness" meaning "blessing.") This assertion St. Paul supports with an allusion to the Ten Commandments, the foundation and heart of the Law: **Honor your father and mother** (Ex. 20:12). If this is done, the Law promises, **it** will **be well with you and you** will **live long on the earth**. That is, you will know the blessing of God as you grow up and your youth will not be cut short.

Fathers are not to **anger** their children. That is, they are not to punish them so strictly that they become discouraged. It is too easy a thing to bruise the heart of a child. A broken spirit is not a help in growing up to be a healthy Christian (see Prov. 18:14)! Rather, as an alternative to worldly ways of discipline, they are to **nurture them**. The word translated **nurture** (Gr. *ektrepho*) is the same word used for the care of one's own body in 5:29. The fathers are thus to care for their children with the same tenderness and care they give to their own selves.

This care is to be exercised as part of their **discipline and admonition**. Discipline (Gr. *paideia*) is the normal word used for training and educating the young; **admonition** (Gr. *nouthesia*) is the word St. Paul regularly uses to describe the correcting and instructing of the flock (see Rom. 15:14; 1 Thess. 5:12). In secular use, these words reflect a rather stringent severity. But St. Paul says the instruction and admonition is to be **of the Lord**—that is, it is to reflect the same loving care that the Lord exercises as He instructs and admonishes us.

ॐ ॐ ॐ ॐ ॐ

5   Slaves, obey your lords according to *the* flesh,
    with fear and trembling, in the singleness of
    heart, as to Christ;
6   not by way of eye-service, as men-pleasers, but
    as slaves of Christ, doing the will of God from
    the soul.
7   Serve *as slaves* with good will, as to the Lord,
    and not to men,
8   knowing that whatever good each one does,
    this he will receive back from the Lord, whether
    he is slave or free.
9   And lords, do the same to them, and leave off
    threatening, knowing that both their Lord and
    yours is in *the* heavens, and there is no respect-
    of-persons with Him.

The relationship of slaves and masters is dealt with next.

Slavery was presupposed in the ancient world and, in St. Paul's day, was as ingrained a part of the social fabric as interest rates are in the economic fabric of today. Though basically inconsistent with the Gospel (the Church's position that "in Christ there is neither slave nor free" [Gal. 3:28] completely undercut the basis of slavery), yet it was still a part of the world inherited by the apostolic Church. The Church was not in a position to immediately change the world. (Indeed, it brought a freedom and dynamic in which questions of changing the world and of slavery and freedom were ultimately irrelevant; see 1 Cor. 7:21–24.) It was necessary then to assume the existence of slavery as a part of the reality of "this world" and to deal with it.

The **slaves** are to **obey** their **lords according to** *the* **flesh**. In using this expression for their earthly masters, St. Paul recognizes that their true Master and Lord is the Lord in heaven. It is to Him that that slave service is truly directed. They are to serve and work **with fear and trembling**—an expression denoting not cringing servility and terror, but profound humility. (St. Paul says that he himself was with the church in Corinth in "much fear and trembling" [1 Cor. 2:3].) They are to perform their tasks **in the singleness of heart**, sincerely, **doing the will of God from the soul**. They can take comfort in knowing that their service is not simply a misfortune imposed by circumstances—it is **the will of God**. That is, it is how they will work out their salvation and please Christ, whose slaves they actually are. Their tasks, though received by their earthly master, are actually an offering to Christ, and whatever **good** thing they do will receive its commensurate reward from Him. Thus, they should not work with mere **eye-service, as men-pleasers**. That is, they should not only work when they are watched and may be rewarded. They should work hard always, for their true Master, the Lord Jesus, always sees them, and there will be true and final recompense from Him. This applies to *all*, **whether slave or free**— even to their masters!

Their **lords** should **do the same to them**. Here is an amazing teaching and one without true parallel in the pagan world. For the pagans, there was a basic difference between slaves and lords, and no true equality between them. Slaves were but living tools. But here St. Paul tells the lords to behave the same as their slaves. That is, he tells them to treat their slaves well, knowing they too will receive a reward from the true Lord of all on the Last Day. They must **leave off threatening** them—a form of lordly behavior taken for granted in the ancient pagan world. Slaves, in fact, must be treated as brethren. There is to be a kind of basic equality between lord and slave, notwithstanding their highly unequal social relation. This underlying equality is based on the fact that both have the same true Lord and Master—the Lord Christ **in *the* heavens**. There is **no respect-of-persons with Him**. Lordly cruelty will be avenged and lordly kindness rewarded.

Thus all relations are to be brought under the transforming power of the Gospel—wives and husbands, children and parents, even slaves and masters. All the relationships of our life are to be a part of our service to Christ.

136

§VII   Exhortation to Stand Fast in Conflict with Darkness (6:10–20)

༄ ༄ ༄ ༄ ༄

10 For the rest, be empowered in *the* Lord and in the might of His strength.

11 Put on the panoply of God, that you may be able to stand against the scheming of the devil.

12 For our wrestling is not against flesh and blood, but against the rulers, against the authorities, against the world-rulers of the darkness of this age, against the spiritual *forces* of evil in the heavenlies.

Realizing the intensity of the spiritual conflict in which all Christians are engaged, St. Paul concludes with an exhortation to stand fast and to win the victory. For the spiritual life does not consist solely of our relationships with other people. It also consists of our struggle against the powers of darkness.

He writes that we are to **be empowered** (Gr. *endunamoo*)—a word cognate with the word for "power" (Gr. *dunamis*). That is, we are to be strong in the power that the Lord provides, the power of the Holy Spirit, and not in our own strength. For the Lord promised us spiritual power through our Pentecostal gift of the Spirit in chrismation. "You will receive power [Gr. *dunamis*]", He said, "when the Holy Spirit has come upon you" (Acts 1:8). If we trust to our own might, wisdom, and willpower, we are doomed to defeat. It is only as we are **empowered** by the Lord that we can **stand against . . . the devil**. For we are not **wrestling** against mere human beings of **flesh and blood**. The cunning and might that opposes us is greater and more deadly. It is the power of the demonic **rulers** and **authorities** (see 3:10) that we face, the **world-rulers** (Gr. *kosmokrator*) of spiritual armies **in the heavenlies**. No wonder that we need the spiritual might of the Lord to withstand this devilish **scheming**.

ॐ ॐ ॐ ॐ ॐ

13 Therefore, take up the panoply of God, so that you may be able to withstand in the evil day, and having achieved all things, to stand.

14 Stand therefore, having girded your loins with truth, and having put on the breastplate of righteousness,

15 and having shod your feet with the equipment of the Gospel of peace;

16 with all *these things*, taking up the shield of faith with which you will be able to quench all the flaming arrows of the evil one.

17 And take the helmet of salvation, and the sword of the Spirit, which is the Word of God.

To stand up and survive the scheming of the devil in **the evil day** (i.e. the day of battle), we need to put on all the armor God provides. This **panoply** is modeled after that worn by the Roman soldiers of St. Paul's day—which soldiers he would have had plenty of opportunity to observe, as he sat guarded by them in prison! The imagery is also suggested by the armor worn by Yahweh in Isaiah 59:17 and Wisdom 5:17–20. There, the Lord puts on righteousness as a breastplate, and salvation as a helmet for His head, putting these on over the mantle of vengeance and fury. He will take holiness as a shield and stern wrath as a sword. These OT images are meant to describe Yahweh going forth to battle to defend righteous Israel against its human foes. Adapting this OT imagery, St. Paul describes the armor which the Christian will use for the battle against his spiritual foes. They will be empowered to remaining **standing** at the battle's end, having **achieved all things** and done all the exploits required of them, if they use all the armor God supplies.

They must **gird** their **loins with truth**. In those days, when one wore long and loose-flowing robes, one had to gird one's loins by gathering the robes around one and tying them with the belt. In the military, this belt was the symbol and insignia of the army. It indicated the willingness to run forward and fight. St. Paul says that the belt which enables us to fight is the **truth** of the Gospel, our faith in Jesus. This **truth** is our military insignia, what makes us part of the Army of Christ.

They must **put on the breastplate of righteousness**. This **righteousness** is the holiness of our life as dedicated soldiers of Christ (see 5:9). Without righteous and holy living, we have no defense to keep our hearts safe. Even as the breastplate protects the soldier's heart, so our walking as the "children of light" (see 5:8) protects us from the power of the enemy. If we partake of the "unfruitful works of darkness" (5:11), we leave ourselves vulnerable and wide open to the enemy.

They must **shoe** their **feet with the equipment of the Gospel of peace**. The soldier had to be shod with good sandals if he was to be mobile enough to march into battle. Roman soldiers especially went all over the world, fighting for their emperor. In the same way, we too must be shod with the willingness to go and preach the Gospel. The image draws upon Isaiah 52:7 (in the LXX version): "How beautiful upon the mountains are the feet of him who announces the good news [Gr. *evaggelizo*—who 'preaches the Gospel'] of peace." In its original OT context, it speaks of the good news of Yahweh's victory and says how welcome are the messengers who run and bring these tidings, how beautiful their feet that have brought such news! In the NT application of this text, it speaks of the Good News of Christ's victory, the Gospel (Gr. *evaggelion*) brought by Christian messengers and preachers. Their feet too are beautiful, bringing such news. In order to go and preach, however, they first must shoe their feet—not with the sandals of soldiers, ready for war, but with **the Gospel of peace**.

With all *these things* (meaning, as supremely important and not to be forgotten), they must take up **the shield of faith**. St. Paul especially stresses this piece of armor because it will be needed to **quench all the flaming arrows of the evil one**. The lethal attacks of the devil are constantly fired at us—assaults from both within and without, both temptations to sin and persecution from the world. Our only defense is **the shield of faith**, which is our trust in God and reliance upon His divine help. The Roman shield, which was the model for this, was quite large, covering the soldier's full torso. It was designed to be large enough to hide behind. In the same way, we can take cover and find safety in the Lord's rescue. "He is our help and our shield" (Ps. 33:20).

They must take **the helmet of salvation**. This piece of armor protected the head, so that the soldier could lift up his head in battle. In St. Paul's description of the Christian's armor in 1 Thessalonians 5:8, he describes this helmet as "the hope of salvation." It is this nuance which is present here also. Trusting in our final salvation, armed with this "hope," we can lift up our heads in all our conflicts. We are defended from depression, discouragement, and being downcast, for we know the Lord will come and save us on the Last Day. As the Lord Himself said in Luke 21:28 concerning our struggle in the final times, "When these things begin to take place, look up and lift up your heads, for your redemption is drawing near!" We can lift up our heads confidently, protected by the hope of our salvation.

Finally, as the only offensive piece of armor, they must take **the sword of the Spirit, which is the Word of God**. This **Word** (Gr. *rema*) is the spoken proclamation of the Gospel. The Romans overcame their foes by killing them with the sword. We overcome ours by converting them with the Gospel. Their weapon is wielded with aggression; ours, with love. (Indeed, swords are sharp, dangerous things, and the sword of the Gospel is much too dangerous to be handled without love.)

Note: in NT usage, the term **the Word of God** refers not to the written Scriptures, but to the spoken and living Word. In this verse it refers therefore to the proclamation of the Gospel, not to the Bible—though obviously the preacher will use the Scriptures in his proclamation.

ॐ ॐ ॐ ॐ ॐ

18 With all prayer and supplication pray at all times in the Spirit, and to this *end,* keep awake

---

> with all perseverance and supplication for all
> the saints,
> 19 and *pray* for me, that a word may be given me
> in the opening of my mouth, to make known
> with boldness the mystery of the Gospel,
> 20 for which I am an ambassador in chains; that
> in speaking it I may be bold, as I ought.

The armor of God presupposes a prayerful life. Indeed, each piece of the panoply is put on by prayer, and without a life of prayer, none of this armor is of any use. So it is that St. Paul exhorts us to **all prayer and supplication**. This **prayer** (Gr. *proseuchs*) is prayer in general, while **supplication** (Gr. *deesis*)is a particular request. That is, they are to keep saying their prayers, praying morning and evening as all the pious did. Within this Rule of Prayer, they are to offer special intercessory petitions. They are not to pray only a while and then give up. Rather, they are to **keep awake with all perseverance** as they continue faithfully to make special requests **for all the saints**.

Note again the corporate aspect of the Faith: their love is not to be bounded and limited to their own little circle. They are to make special supplications for *all* the believers throughout the world, wherever it is heard that there is need.

St. Paul urges them to make this constant prayer **in the Spirit**— that is, to pray fervently, from the inner spirit and heart (see Rom. 1:9), as moved by the Holy Spirit within. St. Paul speaks about the Spirit praying within us, interceding "with groans too deep for words" (Rom. 8:26). This inner fervency, this intense groaning before God, seems to be what is meant. It is thus that we "pray in the Holy Spirit" (Jude 20). They are to intercede with special intensity, as moved and carried by the Spirit within them.

St. Paul asks for such intercessions for himself also, saying **and** *pray* **for me**. (Note that he does not ask for such prayer for himself first. Typically, he takes thought first **for all the saints** and only then, as befitting "the very least of all the saints" [see 3:8], does he ask for himself.) As one languishing in prison before his trial before Caesar, he does not ask for prayer that he be released. This is in the

hands of God and is a matter of comparative indifference to him
(see Phil. 1:21–23). What he asks prayer for is that, when his trial
comes, God will give him **a word**, a special message to help him
make known with boldness the mystery of the Gospel. The temptation, for any Roman citizen, was to be overawed before the great
Caesar, the Master of the World. Yet St. Paul serves Another, the
true Master of the World, and he is under obligation (**ought**) to
speak boldly for Him. He is His **ambassador**, even though he is **in
chains**. These chains might have the effect of cowing the spirit of
any man. Yet St. Paul knows himself to be *not* just "any man," but
an apostle of Christ. Caesar dared the outrage of putting His
ambassador in chains, but St. Paul is not cowed. In humility, he
asks for the intercessions of the Church, so that when the crucial
time comes for **speaking**, he may **be bold** for the Gospel.

§VIII   Final Personal News (6:21–23)

ॐ ॐ ॐ ॐ ॐ

21 But that you also may know the things concerning me, what I am doing, Tychicus, the
   beloved brother and faithful servant in *the* Lord,
   will make everything known to you.
22 I have sent him to you for this very thing, that
   you may know the things concerning us, and
   that he may encourage your hearts.
23 Peace be to the brothers, and love with faith,
   from God the Father and the Lord Jesus Christ.

Normally, a letter would conclude with final and specific greetings. Because this is a circular letter and not one addressed to just
one community, the usual greetings are omitted. Actual greetings
and further personal news can be received from **Tychicus**, the bearer
of the epistle. It is his job, as St. Paul's **beloved brother and faithful
servant in *the* Lord**, to pass along this news as he travels from town
to town, reading the Ephesian circular and distributing other letters

from St. Paul to their destinations. With typical pastoral love, St. Paul's concern is that their **hearts** might be **encouraged** by Tychicus. He, the languishing prisoner, is concerned that they, on the outside, be comforted! Here we see, in this passing and almost unconscious reference, the great heart of the apostle of God.

§IX   Concluding Blessing (6:24)

꣠ ꣠ ꣠ ꣠ ꣠

24 Grace be with all those who love our Lord Jesus Christ with incorruptible *love*.

This final blessing, customary in St. Paul's letters, bears here a special touch. He bids God's grace on the Church and describes the Church as those who **love our Lord . . . with incorruptible *love*.** It not only means that our love for the Lord will not fade in this age and that we will not apostatize from Him. The word **incorruptible** (Gr. aphtharsia) is a strong word, savoring of the final resurrection. (It is used by St. Paul in 1 Cor. 15:53 of the time when "this corruptible body shall put on incorruption.") Its use here means that we, the Church, will continue to love our Lord Jesus Christ, not only in this passing age, but also in the age to come. All the trials of this age will pass—the misery of prison, the temptations to sin, the persecution and struggles with the powers of darkness. All will pass away when our Lord returns to judge the world and to clothe us with incorruption. Our love for Him, begun now, will never cease. We will continue to love Him forever, when we are clothed with immortality and when we rule with Him to the ages of ages.

❧ The Epistle of St. Paul the Apostle to the Colossians ❧

The Church at Colossae

Colossae was a small town in the Lycus Valley which had seen better times. Along with the neighboring cities of Laodicea and Hierapolis, it used to be a mighty and influential city. Certainly it was located in a wealthy area, and its sister cities continued to be prosperous and important. Laodicea was a place of political importance in the area, and Hierapolis was a great trade center with a popular spa. Colossae, on the other hand, retreated into comparative insignificance. Though it was located in the same province of Asia Minor as was Ephesus, where St. Paul spent two years, the apostle never visited Colossae. It was evangelized by Epaphras, St. Paul's convert from that town and its first bishop. (No doubt Epaphras himself heard the Gospel through the extended influence of St. Paul when he taught all Asia Minor from his seat in Ephesus [Acts 19:10].)

When St. Paul was imprisoned in Rome (probably in the spring of AD 61), he was still allowed to receive visitors, and these brought him news of his churches throughout the Roman world. He at length heard from his old convert and friend Epaphras, who told him of the situation in his native Colossae—of their love and faith, but also of problems—notably of the incipient Gnostic heresies which were sweeping through the Lycus Valley.

Gnosticism was a movement which professed secret and saving "knowledge" (Gr. *gnosis*). It was syncretistic, combining Christianity with many other religions and influences. In the Phrygian area around Colossae, it appeared to have a strong Jewish element as well. (Indeed, there was a rabbinical saying that many Jews had left the strictness of Palestinian Judaism for "the wines and baths of Phrygia.") This syncretistic Gnosticism combined a great many disparate elements. Like Judaism, this Colossian strand of Gnosticism stressed the importance of obedience to the Law as an essential element in salvation. The food laws and holy-day regulations seem to have been important in this system, as well as an insistence on circumcision.

But this heresy (unlike that of the Judaizers, which menaced the Galatian and Philippian Christians) was not a simple reversion to Jewish legalism. There were more exotic and theosophic elements in it as well. It would seem that this heresy (like the later and more developed Gnostic systems of which it was a precursor) posited the incompatibility of God with His creation. The holy, invisible, changeless, and bodiless God, the eternal Spirit, could surely not be directly involved with the created material world in all its changeable, visible, and bodily ambiguity! The created world was . . . well, so "yucky"! People were conceived in brute passion and born in blood, lived in pain, and died in ignorance, again dissolving into slime. Surely the true God would have nothing directly to do with all this! So the Gnostic movement, in all its varied forms, posited the divine "fullness" as a series of emanations, each one derived from its predecessor and a little more distant from the original divine "center." And also, a little more *ignorant* of the original divine center! (Indeed, one later Gnostic text suggested that when the God of the Old Testament declared Himself in Isaiah 45:6 to be the only God, He was mistaken and was rebuked as blindly sinning against the rest of the divine "fullness," i.e. the other gods.) In this Gnostic understanding of the Godhead, Christ was perhaps but the last "link" in the divine chain stretching from the original "center" down to the created world. Thus the original true God did not have to be directly involved in the material world, but was only related to it through a long series of mediating "emanations" (or "eons"). It would appear that these Gnostics considered that the angelic "principalities and authorities" had their place in this divine "fullness" and that they were to be worshipped (like Christ, who was also considered to be one of the angelic "eons").

Obviously, such a movement, which professed a kind of philosophical "snob appeal," was utterly alien to the apostolic Gospel! When Epaphras brought St. Paul news of its popularity in the Lycus

Valley, the apostle was moved to write to the Colossians under Epaphras' care so that they would not be "deluded by smooth-talk" (2:4), but would be filled with a truly spiritual wisdom to lead a life worthy of the Lord (1:9, 10).

There was also another potential crisis in Colossae that St. Paul wanted to deal with. While preaching the Gospel to many from his prison cell in Rome (see Acts 28:30, 31; Phil. 1:13), he had made a convert of a runaway slave as well. This slave, Onesimus by name, had been owned by Philemon, who, with his wife Apphia, opened their home to their fellow Christians and hosted one of the weekly eucharistic gatherings of the church in Colossae. (Philemon was perhaps one of the presbyter-bishops there, one of the local Colossian clergy.) Onesimus had fled from Philemon (a capital offense in those days) and at length found his way to the large anonymity of the Roman metropolis. There, by the providence of God, he was converted through the preaching of St. Paul. Though the apostle would have liked to keep Onesimus with him, he knew too that he must return home to Philemon to "face the music." So it was that St. Paul wrote a brief letter also to his dear friend Philemon, urging him to receive Onesimus back into his home and into his heart, forgiving him as a beloved fellow-brother in Christ (Philemon 17). He even hints that perhaps Philemon might "do even more than I say" (v. 21)—i.e. grant Onesimus his freedom.

These two epistles bound for Colossae (one for the church at large there and the other for Philemon in particular) were entrusted to Tychicus (St. Paul's friend and contact in Rome) along with Onesimus (4:7–9). Tychicus was to deliver all the letters bound for that area—a letter to the Ephesians (which was coming as a circular letter to the Colossians as well, by way of Laodicea; see 4:16) along with the two letters bound specifically for Colossae. These two Colossian epistles were written (perhaps) in the spring of 62. St. Paul expected soon to be tried and acquitted, at which time he hoped to visit them himself (Philemon 22). His trial did indeed come in the spring of 63, after which he was found innocent and released.

These two Colossian epistles, both brief, are a lasting tribute to the apostle's care for the small and outwardly insignificant. Colossae

was but a small town and Onesimus but one slave among the many
thousands of slaves in the Roman Empire. Nonetheless, the great
apostle, in the midst of his own imprisonment and tribulation, takes
thought for these. In doing so, he leaves us a priceless monument of
Christological teaching and of the Christian love which transcends
every barrier—even that between slave and lord.

❦ The Epistle to the Colossians ❧

§I   Opening Greetings (1:1, 2)

❧ ❧ ❧ ❧ ❧

1 1   Paul, an apostle of Christ Jesus by the will of
God, and Timothy our brother,

    2   To the saints and faithful brethren in Christ
who are at Colossae: Grace to you and peace
from God our Father.

As in other epistles, St. Paul puts his apostolic authority promi-
nently in the fore, to give weight to the exhortations that follow.
This **will of God** is that which violently took him from being a
persecutor of the Church to being the humbled and faithful disciple of **Christ Jesus** and His chosen vessel to bring the Gospel to
the Gentiles (Acts 9:1ff; 26:16–18). St. Paul never forgot his conversion experience, for it was the foundation not only of his authority but also of his humility. Though he was unworthy to be called
an apostle because of his persecution of the Church (1 Cor. 15:9),
nevertheless the Lord had called him to it and he never forgot this
lesson in humility.

It is his usual practice to include **Timothy** as joint author of his
epistles, including him, as it were, in the apostolic circle. In this also
we see his humility as well as the conciliarity of the Faith, which
resists individuality, even in the apostolate.

❧ ❧ ❧ ❧ ❧

§II   Opening Thanksgiving—for their faith, love, and hope (1:3–8)

ॐ॰ ॐ॰ ॐ॰ ॐ॰ ॐ॰

3 We give thanks to God, the Father of our Lord
   Jesus Christ, always praying for you,
4 having heard of your faith in Christ Jesus and
   the love which you have for all the saints;
5 because of the hope laid up for you in the heavens, of which you heard-before in the Word of
   the truth of the Gospel
6 which has come to you, as in all the world also
   it is fruit-bearing and growing, even as it has
   been doing among you also since *the* day you
   heard and really-knew the grace of God in truth;
7 as you learned it from Epaphras, our beloved
   fellow-slave, who is a faithful servant of Christ
   on our behalf,
8 and he also made plain to us your love in the
   Spirit.

As in all letters of that time, St. Paul begins with an opening
thanksgiving. He gives thanks for faith, love, and hope—a favorite
combination in St. Paul's thought (see e.g. 1 Cor. 13:13). Their
faith is in Christ; their **love** is directed towards **all the saints** (and
not just those of their own little circle of acquaintance). This is
sustained and has its roots in the **Word of the truth**—the original
Gospel message they heard proclaimed by Epaphras. This Word
told them also of their **hope**—that is, "the hope of glory" (1:27),
the hope and certainty of glory in the age to come, **laid up** and kept
safe for them **in the heavens**. For Christ sits enthroned in the heavens, at the right hand of God, and He is their certainty of future
glory. This they have **heard-before**. By saying that they have already
heard all of this before through Epaphras, St. Paul stresses the continuity of this message with their original Gospel. For the heretics

(of whom he will warn them in his letter) would give them teaching *not* consistent with the Gospel they originally received. It is important for them to continue along the path once-for-all laid out for them (see 2:6).

He continues to stress the continuity of his message with the Gospel they have already received. One characteristic of heresy is its *local* character, for each heresy is the personal interpretation and individual thought of *one person*. As such, it inevitably has a local, regional following only. The true Gospel, on the other hand, is proclaimed by *all* the apostles where they have been scattered throughout all the world. Thus one can distinguish the false and heretical from the true Faith by the test of universality: whatever was, at that early time, found throughout the world was the true apostolic Faith. And what St. Paul is preaching to them is also found **fruit-bearing and growing in all the world**. It is this true and universal Catholic Faith which is bearing fruit in them also. Their experience is a genuine participation in this worldwide movement. It is through this that they have come to **really-know** [Gr. *epiginosko*] **the grace of God in truth**. The word translated (a bit awkwardly) *really-know* is cognate with the Greek word *epignosis*—not just "knowledge" (Gr. *gnosis*) but true and intimate knowledge (*epignosis)*. That is, the Colossians, through the Gospel, have not just come to a superficial acquaintance with the power and grace of God. They have a deep and abiding experience of it **in truth**.

St. Paul acknowledges a spiritual foundation soundly laid by Epaphras, his colleague and fellow-worker (**fellow-slave**) in the apostolate. It was from him that they **learned** of God's grace—through him that they became the Lord's disciples. St. Paul takes care here to stress the connection he has with their own founder, Epaphras. Epaphras is, in fact, a **beloved fellow-slave** with St. Paul, but also **a faithful servant of Christ on** Paul's **behalf**. That is, it was through St. Paul's influence that Epaphras himself was converted (see Acts 19:10), so that Epaphras' ministry might even be considered to be an extension of St. Paul's own. It is because of this close connection with their own Epaphras that Paul now has the courage to exhort and direct those he has never actually met or converted.

Besides, Epaphras himself **made plain** to him their situation in the first place. It is through him that St. Paul thought to write them at all!

§III   Opening Prayer—for them to know God's will and be strengthened to persevere (1:9–12)

ॐ॰ ॐ॰ ॐ॰ ॐ॰ ॐ॰

9   Therefore, we *ourselves* also, from the day we heard *of it*, have not ceased to pray for you, asking that you may be filled with the real-knowledge of His will in all spiritual wisdom and insight,

10   to walk worthily of the Lord, pleasing Him in all things, bearing-fruit in every good work and growing in the real-knowledge of God;

11   empowered with all power, according to the might of His glory, for all perseverance and patience; with joy

12   giving thanks to the Father, who has qualified us for our portion of the inheritance of the saints in the Light,

---

As with many letters in antiquity, St. Paul also begins with an opening prayer for the recipients. He prays, and has always prayed, since the day he heard of their conversion through his own convert Epaphras, that they **may be filled with the real-knowledge** [Gr. *epignosis*)] **of His will**. The Gnostic movement professes an elite and secret knowledge (Gr. *gnosis*) of the hidden mysteries, but here is the *true* and real knowledge. This true knowledge has an ethical component to it. It is not merely a knowledge for the head (which tends to puff up with conceit, see 1 Cor. 8:1). It is a knowledge for the heart and the life; it is a knowledge of how to live, of **His will** for a holy life. As such, it is **in all spiritual wisdom and insight**. Wisdom is a word with a long history in the Scriptures. It does not mean merely a worldly shrewdness, but an understanding of the hidden ways of God. In the prayer here it has a moral aspect to it—

our knowledge of God involves knowing what kind of a God He is—and therefore how He wants us to live also. It is coupled here with **insight**. In the present context, this word also has a moral flavor to it—we are to insightfully discern how to **please** God and give His heart joy **in all things**. This is what it means to **walk worthily of the Lord**. His holy and ineffable Name has been called over us and He has claimed us as His own. His honor is, in some way, bound up with our own, so that for us to live dishonorably would be to dishonor *Him*. Thus ours is no cold "ethic," no prim and proper frigidity of the heart which retreats from sin in icy self-righteousness. Rather, ours is the zealous striving to walk worthily of the Lord and Lover of our souls; it is the warmhearted love of children who seek to please their Father.

This holiness and **real-knowledge** for which St. Paul prays is also no static thing. It is constantly **bearing-fruit** and producing good works of every kind. One filled with the knowledge of God overflows with joy, love, and peace, with almsgiving and acts of mercy. The world around them can see and taste the fruit of the Lord (see Eph. 5:9). (There can thus be no real dichotomy between personal piety and social consciousness.) Also, the one with **real-knowledge** of God **grows** and increases, maturing into an ever-greater **real-knowledge** of God. It is not just that we now, once and for all, have come to know God. Knowledge of the Most High is an eternal upward spiral. However much we know of Him and His love, there is always more to know. His love (to change the image) is a depth which no man can fathom. Age will succeed age as we continue to discover more of God's love.

Finally, this experience of growth is not the result of our own puny willpower. Rather, we are to be **empowered with all power** [Gr. *en pase dunamei dunamoumenoi*], **according to the might of His glory**. This is, in fact, a reference to the power of the Holy Spirit, though His Name is not mentioned. For He is the One who is the source of our power (see Luke 24:49). Through the Spirit, all the **might of** God's **glory**—that is, all the glorious might which God showed when He raised Christ from the dead (see Eph. 1:19, 20)—is now given to us. The power of Christ's invincible

Resurrection is to be working in us, helping us to **persevere** with **patience**. Whatever obstacles meet us, we can overcome them, remaining steadfast through any adversity, **empowered with all** the **power** of the resurrected Lord.

St. Paul mentions something that separates the patient perseverance of the Christian from that of the pagan Stoic. For the ancient Stoics (a philosophical sect) stressed patience also. Their aim was to achieve self-sufficiency, to be unmoved by any disaster, serene and sane in a crazy world. It was a laudable aim. But the Stoic patience lacked one thing: the exuberant joy of the Lord. St. Paul prays that their patience may be joined with joy—that they may not only be **patient**, but may **give thanks with joy**.

This is, of course, a liturgical reference. In their weekly Eucharists, the Colossians **give thanks** [Gr. *eucharisteo*] **with joy to the Father**, who **qualified** them through their baptism so that they might have a **portion**, on the Last Day, in the eternal **inheritance of the saints in the Light**. But this joyful thanksgiving is not to be confined to their Sunday Eucharists. St. Paul here prays that this may be their constant experience, their daily rule and privilege. And their joy will come as they contemplate their future. They are to have their **portion** in the coming Kingdom of God. Now, in this age, is the time of darkness (see Eph. 6:12, which speaks of "this present darkness"). With the Second Coming of Christ will come the final triumph of the **Light**, and the time when all the **saints** and true believers will at last enjoy their promised **inheritance**. Their baptism **qualifies** them for their **portion** in that coming Kingdom. So it is that they can give thanks **with joy** as they anticipate the final reward of grace.

§IV   The Cosmic Christ and His Salvation (1:13–23)

St. Paul continues to describe their salvation (for which their baptism qualified them) and the cosmic Savior and Lord who won it for them. The following passage continues without a grammatical break from the previous prayer, as St. Paul's enthusiasm carries him off in one of his (usual) long sentences.

ॐ ॐ ॐ ॐ ॐ

13 who rescued us from the authority of darkness,
    and removed us to the Kingdom of the Son of
    His love,
14 in whom we have redemption, the forgiveness
    of sins,

St. Paul describes their salvation as being **rescued from the authority of darkness**. Prior to their knowing Christ, they lived under the tyranny of Satan, "the god of this world" (2 Cor. 4:4), the ruler of the darkness of this present age (see Eph. 2:2). Now, Christ has **rescued** them, snatching them, as it were, from the jaws of death. Through their baptism they have been **removed to the Kingdom** of God's beloved Son. The word translated *removed* (Gr. *methistemi*) is the word used for the removal of peoples from one nation to another. In the ancient world, when a nation was conquered, the conquering king would often remove entire segments of the population and transplant them, as permanent exiles, to his own land. (Thus were many of the Jews removed from Palestine and brought as exiles to Babylon by Nebuchadnezzar; see 2 Kings 24:10–17.) Thus they became citizens of a new country, with a loyalty to a new king (and so were less likely to plot rebellion at home!). It is this concept that St. Paul uses here. God **rescued** us from Satan's land, where we had been held prisoners, and **removed** us to our new home-land—and to no hostile foreign country (as the Jews found Babylon), but to our true and native land—the **Kingdom** of Christ (**the Son of His love**—a very Jewish expression for the Messiah).

Thus we have been entirely liberated from the power of Satan, having left the land of our former bondage far behind. For in Christ we have **redemption, the forgiveness of sins**. This last is said with one eye upon the Gnostic heresy. The Gnostics saw redemption primarily in terms of "knowledge" (Gr. *gnosis*), consisting of a series of secret passwords which would enable them, after death, to pass up through all the eons and divine emanations to their final salvation. It was very much a matter of secret occult lore. On the contrary, St. Paul here asserts, redemption is not a matter of secret knowledge, but of the **forgiveness of sins**. It is given freely, by Christ Himself, at our baptism, abundantly bestowed now upon all. We do not have to busy ourselves with theosophical secrets, but simply receive God's gift with an open and penitent heart.

ॐ ॐ ॐ ॐ ॐ

15 who is the image of the invisible God, the first-born of all creation,

16 for in Him all things were created, in the heavens and on earth, visible and invisible, whether thrones or dominions or rulers or authorities— all things were created through Him and for Him

17 and *it is* He *who* is before all things, and in Him all things hold-together,

---

The reference to Christ, the messianic Son of God's love, leads St. Paul to further describe the Lord. For the Gnostics did not just misunderstand the nature of our salvation. They misunderstood (rather willfully) the nature of the Savior Himself. For them, He was but one link in the divine chain, connecting the central and inner Godhead with the material creation. Between this Godhead and the world was a great and lengthy series of "eons," emanations, and mediators. Far from the central Godhead, as but one link in the chain, was the inferior and deluded God of the Old Testament. The angels had their places in this emanating "fullness" also, as did Christ. With such heresy as this floating about in the popular spiritual culture of the day, no wonder St. Paul felt he should clarify exactly who the Son is!

He begins by describing Christ's position in creation. He is, St. Paul insists, not simply a created being like the rest of us, but rather the **image** [Gr. *eikon*] **of the invisible God**. An image is something visible, a tangible and representative manifestation of its prototype. God, of course, is by nature **invisible**—no one has seen Him nor can see Him (1 Tim. 6:16). Christ, St. Paul says here, is this invisible God made visible, the manifestation of God in human flesh. As the Lord Himself said, "He who has seen Me has seen the Father" (John 14:9). Not, of course, that He *is* the Father. Rather, the Father is the Father and the Son is the Son; the two are distinct; the Son can pray to the Father and submit to His will (see Mark 14:36). Nonetheless, there is a unity between the two. The Father, from all eternity, pours Himself into the Son, the Divine *Logos* and Word, so that the Son has forever been the personal hypostatic manifestation of the Father, the Mirror and Mind (as it were) of the Divine and Paternal Source. The Son continued this manifestation of the Father on earth, in new lowliness, through the Incarnation. It is in this sense that He is **the image of the invisible God**—for to see Him is to see all the fullness of the Father—all the paternal character, righteousness, love, and power (see John 17:6).

He is also **the firstborn** [Gr. *prototokos*] **of all creation**. The term does not mean that Christ was the first thing to be created. (St. Paul already ruled out that possibility when He described Him as the **image of the invisible God**.) Rather, the term **firstborn** was a term of honor, especially in Jewish culture. It signified the favored one and heir. (Thus Israel was described as Yahweh's "firstborn son" in Ex. 4:22, as was the Davidic king in Ps. 89:27.) Its use in the text here means that, of all the beings in **creation**, both men and angels, Christ is the highest, the favored one, the divine heir. He is unique among His fellowmen in being absolutely preeminent over all.

This is because **in Him all things were created**. He is not, as the Gnostics allege, simply one of the angels, one link in the chain of the divine fullness and lower than the other angelic "eons." On the contrary, all of the angels were actually created by Him! The Father created everything through the Son, the divine Word (John 1:3; 1 Cor. 8:6)—not just the **visible** creation of the world around us, but also the **invisible** creation of all the angelic orders—the **thrones, dominions, rulers**, and **authorities**. These terms for the angelic powers St. Paul draws from contemporary Judaism. It is doubtful that we should feel able from this to construct a comprehensive list of the angelic hierarchies. Rather, St. Paul's point seems here to be only that all the angelic orders—even the highest **thrones** and **dominions**—were created by Christ. He is exalted as preeminent above all of creation, as the One **through** whom all things were created and **for** whom they were created. They (and we) were created for His pleasure. (Note: We were not made to pursue our own independent goals, but rather **for Him**. He is the goal and focus of our existence.)

As such, He is also **before all things**, antecedent and prior to all. None can look down on Him as a younger brother in creation. The word **He** is emphatic in the Greek: it does not simply say, "He is before all things," but rather, *it is* **He** Himself, Christ and none other, *who* **is before all things**. The Lord predates all and is superior to all, having seen everything come into being. It is He, in fact, in whom **all things hold-together**. That is, He is the force, principle, and power which makes the entire cosmos co-inhere; it is through Him alone that the universe is upheld (Heb. 1:3).

This view of Christ, received by St. Paul as a part of the total apostolic deposit of the Faith, is a very different picture from the one painted by the Gnostics!

ॐ ॐ ॐ ॐ ॐ

18 and *it is* He *who* is the Head of the Body, the Church; and He is the beginning, the firstborn from the dead, that He Himself might hold the first place in all things,

19 for in Him all the Fullness was pleased to dwell,

20 and through Him to reconcile all things to Himself, having made-peace through the Blood of His Cross; through Him, whether things on the earth or things in the heavens.

St. Paul goes on to describe Christ's position in the Church. He **holds the first place** not only in this present creation but in the redeemed and new creation as well, so that He presides over **all things**. It is not that He is Lord in this present age only, and will be superseded in the age to come by a higher name. No; rather He remains **first** in power and honor forever, both in this age and in the age to come. Once again, the **He** is emphatic in the Greek. St. Paul says that it is Christ—He and none other—the One who is first in this age—who is also first in the next. (Note that St. Paul's discussion of Christ and the age to come is carried out under the heading of Christ and *the Church*. This is significant, for it means that the Church is not just an earthly society of people, assembled for religious purposes. The Church is more than that: it is the presence in this age of the age to come, the foretaste and advance manifestation of the coming eschatological Kingdom. That is why, when St. Paul discusses Christ's supremacy in the age to come, he begins by discussing His supremacy as Head within **the Body, the Church**. For St. Paul, the Church is itself an eschatological reality.)

Christ, St. Paul says, is **the Head of the Body**. That is, He is the source of life for the Church, even as the body was thought to draw its life and direction from the head. He is also **the beginning** (Gr. *arche*), the origin and source of resurrection life in the age to come. That is because He is Himself **the firstborn from the dead**. Once again, the term **firstborn** means that He holds the position of favor and honor, as the divine heir. In the resurrection **from the dead**, He reigns as supreme also. Note: it is not just that Christ was the first one to be raised from the dead. It is more than that: His resurrection on the third day is the source and fount for the final future resurrection. This is as it should be, for **in Him all the Fullness was pleased to dwell**.

The term **Fullness** seems to have been a term favored by the early Gnostics. Certainly it would become a technical term for the divine emanations and series of eons in the future Gnostic systems. St. Paul here says that all the Divine Fullness—the entire Godhead of the Father—**was pleased to dwell** in Christ. This is, of course, a reference to the Incarnation. It does *not* mean that, from all eternity, it was the Father's voluntary decision that His Fullness should dwell in the Son as Their pre-Incarnation mode of existing. St. Paul is not referring to the internal relations of the Holy Trinity. Those relations are not the result of God's voluntary will so much as His eternal Being. God did not "decide" to be the Trinity, as Arius seems to have thought! Rather, St. Paul is referring to our experience of Christ and salvation. He means that it was the Father's voluntary decision to send His Son, the expression of His nature, to become incarnate for us through the Holy Virgin. The cognate of the word *was pleased* (Gr. *eudokeo*) is elsewhere used by St. Paul to mean the "good-pleasure" of God, His "resolve" (Gr. *eudokia*) to send Christ as our Savior (see Eph. 1:5). Similarly, the word *to dwell* (Gr. *katoikeo*) means "to inhabit," as in one dwelling in tents (see its use for Abraham "dwelling" in tents [Heb. 11:9]). Here it refers to Christ becoming incarnate and "pitching His tent" among us (John 1:14). Christ, St. Paul says, was not the last link of a long series. He was the totality of Godhead, as all the Divine Fullness, by the good-pleasure and will of God, became incarnate in Him.

Thus, through Christ as the Fullness of the Father, God has **reconciled all things to Himself.** Note that this includes both **things on the earth** and **things in the heavens.** The redemption is cosmic in scope, including both men and angels. Again with one eye on the Gnostics, St. Paul says that it is not the case that the heavenly eons are superior to Christ; rather, all the heavenly powers find their peace through Him as their Reconciler and Savior! We should not conclude from this, however, that the angels needed reconciliation to God as we sinners do, nor that Christ died for the sins of the angels. Indeed, Scripture explicitly tells us that He became incarnate *not* for the angels, but solely for us, human children and seed of Abraham (Heb. 2:14–17). Rather, this means that our sin has affected the entire creation, subjecting it to involuntary bondage (Rom. 8:20, 21). The whole universe is out of joint and there is war in heaven (Rev. 12:7). As Blessed Theodoret says, it is not so much that the angels were reconciled to God as that they were reconciled *to us!* For **peace** has been made **through the Blood of His Cross,** restoring harmony to the cosmos.

We see from this how great and cosmic is our salvation. Christ did not just die for men, to save our souls so that we could go to heaven. It is better and grander than that. Christ's Blood has washed the whole world, restoring all to its original pristine beauty and freshness, making all things new (Rev. 21:5). We men have our share in this salvation, since man is the microcosm of the world. But the fact remains that Christ's death brought the whole cosmos back into life-giving unity with the Father—not just us!

ॐ ॐ ॐ ॐ ॐ

21 And you *yourselves* who once were estranged and enemies in the mind by evil works,

22 He has now reconciled in the body of His flesh through death, to present you before Him holy and blameless and irreproachable—

23 if indeed you remain on in the Faith founded and firm, and not shifting from the hope of the Gospel that you heard, which was heralded in all creation under the heaven, and of which I, Paul, became a servant.

St. Paul at last comes to describe their salvation in this cosmic Christ. As Gentiles, they were **estranged** from the commonwealth of Israel, from God's mighty acts and from His life (see Eph. 2:12). This was because they were **enemies in the mind**. The word translated *mind* (Gr. *dianoia*) means their understanding, their thoughts and basic attitudes (see Eph. 4:18). Their **mind** was set on the flesh; they were completely self-engrossed and so were hostile to God (see Rom. 8:7), contemptuously spurning His love, producing **evil works** which angered Him and invited His righteous judgment.

Yet even so, God has **reconciled** them **in the body of** Christ's **flesh through death**. God's compassion and love refused to return evil for evil, but reached out through Christ even to these **enemies**, reconciling them to Himself through Christ's death on the Cross. Note that St. Paul does not simply say that they were reconciled "in His body through death," but rather the stronger **in the body of His flesh through death**. The physicality and materiality of the Lord's fleshly body is stressed. For the Gnostics despised the physical realm as unworthy of a truly spiritual Deity and denied that the true God would soil Himself by touching such a grossly material world as ours. Indeed, some Gnostics denied that Christ left any footprints! In refutation of such fantasies, St. Paul affirms the full and true Incarnation of the Lord—that Christ our true God, in whom all the Fullness of Deity was pleased to dwell, did indeed assume a fleshly body like ours and truly suffer death. He was not a phantom or a mere apparition. His **death** on the Cross was bloody, painful, and real. Human physicality was thus not something of which to be ashamed. Rather, it was the instrument of our salvation. The Gnostics retreated in revulsion from the flesh as if it were something unworthy. For them, there was a great dichotomy between flesh and spirit. But this was an error: for the Incarnation of Christ dissolved this dichotomy, making the flesh spiritual and making the physical world a channel of divine grace.

The word translated **present** (Gr. *paristemi*) has here a sacrificial flavor. It can mean simply "to be introduced" (as when Paul was "presented" to the governor by the Roman soldiers, Acts 23:33). But in St. Paul's normal usage, there is also a nuance of being presented as a sacrificial offering to God. Thus St. Paul tells the Roman Christians to "present their bodies as a living sacrifice to God" (Rom. 12:1), and he says that he will "present" his converts to Christ on the Last Day (2 Cor. 11:2) as if they were his priestly offering to God (Rom. 15:16). He says that he strives to teach them in all wisdom, so that he may "present" them to God as "perfect" (Col. 1:28), as an offering which is holy and acceptable. Though the apostle of course has his part in this "presentation" and offering of the Church to God, the work is itself the work of God. In some sense, it is *God* who offers us, even though the work in this age is done through His servants. Thus it is said that God will present the believers on the Last Day (2 Cor. 4:14) and that Christ will present the Church to Himself (Eph. 5:27). Thus St. Paul says here that God has reconciled us through Christ's death **to present** us to Himself **holy and blameless and irreproachable**, beyond any charge, accusation, or guilt. As the priests of the Old Covenant took care to present only holy sacrifices to God, so the Lord Himself will present us holy and spotless. Through Christ's death, we may stand before Him on the Last

Day with full confidence and joy, completely forgiven. Once again, it is not a matter of laboriously learning secret Gnostic passwords. Rather, it is a matter of being forgiven through the Cross of Christ.

Their salvation is not now assured. It is conditional upon their **remaining on in the Faith** and not being **shifted from the hope of the Gospel that** they **heard**. Fidelity to the apostolic Tradition is required—if they hearken to Gnostic perversions of the Faith, they cannot hope for this salvation. It is required that they continue to be **founded** and **firm**. The word translated *founded* (Gr. *themelioo*) is cognate with the word for "foundation" (Gr. *themelios*, see Eph. 3:17). That is, they are required to remain on the spiritual foundation once-for-all laid by the apostles. They must be **firm** (Gr. *edraios*), fixed and settled, immovable from their spot (see its use in 1 Cor. 15:58). If they move from this Faith, they move also from their hope in the Gospel. For heresy is not simply a wrong answer or a theological misunderstanding. It is a spiritual treason, a sellout, a betrayal of the Christ they know for the sake of something more fashionable. This Faith they have pledged themselves to has been **heralded** by the apostles **in all creation under the heaven** (unlike the Gnostic movement, which was then a local fashion). This apostolic Faith is obviously the true one—how can they even think of casting it away?

§V   St. Paul Their Servant of This Mystery (1:24–29)

ॐ ॐ ॐ ॐ ॐ

24 Now I rejoice in my sufferings for your sake, and in my flesh I fill up what is lacking in Christ's tribulations on behalf of His Body, which is the Church,

25 of which I became a servant according to the stewardship from God given me for you, so that I might fulfill the Word of God,

Mention of the Faith "heralded" (Gr. *kerusso*) throughout all creation leads St. Paul to think of his own apostolate, for he was appointed to be one of God's "heralds" (Gr. *kerux*; see 1 Tim. 2:7). That is, he was appointed one of His **servants** according to the **stewardship** (Gr. *oikonomia*; see its use in Eph. 1:10) given him from God. His apostolate was not given to him for his own self-aggrandizement, but for the sake of the Gospel. His whole life has been given up for the service of this mystery. He lives now only to serve. His servanthood is apparent in his present experience: **now** (as he sits in his Roman imprisonment) he rejoices in his **sufferings for** their **sake**. His imprisonment sufferings are not a source of mourning or grief for him. On the contrary, he **rejoices** in them— for his sufferings are one more way of serving the Church.

St. Paul here assumes a great and indissoluble unity between Christ and **His Body, which is the Church**. The Church is destined to suffer in this world, for this fact (necessitated by the nature of a holy Church in an unholy world) was spoken by the Lord Himself (e.g. John 15:20). Thus, a certain experience of tribulation is required of Christ's Body worldwide. These **tribulations** (Gr. *thlipsis*, see John 16:33) are spoken of as **Christ's tribulations** because the Church suffers on account of her Master, the Body suffering for its Head. (Thus, when the unconverted persecutor Saul persecuted the Church, the Lord said, "Saul, Saul, why are you persecuting *Me*?" [Acts 9:4]. The sufferings of the Church were counted by the Lord as His *own* sufferings, as the Head suffered in His members.) In every generation then, the Church must suffer. If it does not, it is as if these tribulations were yet **lacking** and still to come. St. Paul here says that his sufferings in Rome are on behalf of the churches, as they **fill up** and supply this lack. Thus the Church's necessary suffering is fulfilled in the apostle's own **flesh**. In this way too he proves himself a **servant** according to the apostolic **stewardship** given him by God (see 1 Cor. 4:1).

This **stewardship** is thus given **for you**—for the Colossians and all the faithful everywhere—since he suffers **for** their **sake**. And it is given to him so that he **might fulfill the Word of God**, the proclamation of the Gospel. He **fulfills** the Word when he preaches it and brings men to receive it (see Rom. 15:19, where he says that he "fulfilled the Gospel of Christ from Jerusalem to Illyricum"). His sufferings were not unfruitful. Through them all he brought more men to the knowledge of Christ (see Phil. 1:12) and so **fulfilled the Word of God.**

⅜ ⅜ ⅜ ⅜ ⅜

26 the mystery hidden from the ages and the generations, but now manifested to His saints,

27 to whom God willed to make known what *is* the riches of the glory of this mystery among the Gentiles, which is Christ among you, the hope of glory.

28 whom we *ourselves* proclaim, admonishing every man and teaching every man in all wisdom, so that we may present every man perfect in Christ.

The Word of God which St. Paul has been called to preach is now further defined as **the mystery hidden** from past **ages and generations.** A *mystery* (Gr. *musterion*), in biblical usage, is not something inexplicable (as in our modern usage). Rather, it is a term given to a secret long hidden but now revealed to the initiated. The Gospel's true import, St. Paul says, has been hidden in the deep counsels of God for the past ages of the Old Testament and only now has been **manifested to His saints,** the true believers in Jesus. As the Lord Himself said to the Twelve, "Many prophets and kings desired to see what you see and did not see it" (Luke 10:24). But now, by the **will** and providential decision of God, the Gospel has come and the **riches of the glory of this mystery** (that is, the overwhelming glory and splendor of the Gospel) have been revealed in the midst of the earth, even before all the nations, **among the Gentiles.** For the glory of this **mystery** is that it even includes **the Gentiles** as co-equal heirs of God's promises—a "new creation" has been created in the earth, one that transcends categories of Jew and Gentile (see Eph. 3:5, 6). Alongside their Jewish Christian brothers, the Gentile Colossian Christians have also been initiated into this **mystery**. And the mystery is this: **Christ among you**, Christ in your midst, **the hope of glory**.

This was the **mystery** long hidden from the world in the secret counsels of God and the wisdom that Israel did not expect. Israel expected the Jewish Messiah to come, to exalt the Jews to a place of prominence in the world (with the Gentiles as their servants), and to reign physically from the city of Jerusalem. The full glory and political prominence would come with the first appearance of the Messiah. (That was what the Jewish crowds were expecting when they welcomed the Lord into Jerusalem on that fateful Palm Sunday; see Mark 11:10.) They did not suspect the **riches of the glory** of God's mystery, or the overflowing generosity of His grace. They did not suspect that God would pour out His grace upon *all flesh*— even the Gentiles, thereby abolishing the distinction between Jew and Gentile.

This is done through the sacramental Presence of Christ with them by His Spirit. He was not to reign physically in Jerusalem— He is to be **among** them, in their midst (Gr. *en umin*), dwelling in their hearts. He comes and "makes His home with them" (John 14:23), indwelling them spiritually. It is *thus* that Christ is in our midst—not by a physical Presence, but by a sacramental and spiritual one. For where two or three of His are gathered together, there He is "in the midst of them" (Matt. 18:20). This spiritual Presence is their **hope of glory**. St. Paul means that the messianic glory is received in **hope** (see Rom. 8:24, 25). Christ's sacramental Presence in their midst is the pledge and promise of their full and future **glory**. They have not received the fullness of messianic glory now. That will be their final reward in the age to come. Now, in this age, the Kingdom of God is present as a **mystery**, as a seed, as a sacrament, sign, and promise. It is this which was not foreseen by the Jews, but which is now, through the apostles, **made known . . . among the Gentiles**.

It is this Christ whom the apostles proclaim. And they take care, wherever they go "in all creation under the heaven" (v. 23), to **admonish** and **teach every man** to **present** him **perfect** on the Last Day. The phrase **every man** is repeated thrice: St. Paul says that the apostles **admonish every man** and **teach every man** in all wisdom, in order to **present every man** perfect in Christ. The emphasis on **every man** is in conscious opposition to the Gnostics. For the Gnostics asserted a secret teaching, transmitted only to the elite. (Later Gnostics would suggest that the apostles taught a humbler, more elementary version of the Faith to the common man, while reserving the secret, advanced teaching for the more spiritual ones—namely, the Gnostics themselves!)

In opposition to this incipient elitism, St. Paul asserts that the apostles teach the whole Gospel to **every man**—there is nothing held back in reserve for a secret group. **Every man**—from the common humble believer to the supposedly more advanced—is given the same admonition. All are taught the same thing, in **all wisdom** (the supposedly advanced wisdom is not reserved for a special group). All will, if they but "remain on in the Faith" (v. 23), be **presented perfect** (Gr. *teleios*) in Christ on the Last Day, as a spotless sacrificial offering (see v. 22). Through obedience to the apostolic Gospel, all can be complete in Christ—they can stand, at the last, fully assured of their salvation, forgiveness, and acceptance. The Gnostics have nothing to add to them.

ॐ ॐ ॐ ॐ ॐ

29 For this also I toil, contesting according to His working, which works in me with power.

St. Paul, with his characteristic modesty, adds himself at the end of his description of apostolic labor. The apostles proclaim, admonish, and teach—and he does too. The term **toil** (Gr. *kopio*) is a strong one, meaning "to labor to the point of exhaustion"—not just to work, but to spend all one's strength (see Phil. 2:16). St. Paul thus asserts that, as a true apostle, he also labors with all his might.

Yet he does this, **contesting according to His working**. The word translated (a bit awkwardly) *contesting* (Gr. *agonizomai*) is cognate with the word *agon*, meaning "contest, struggle, fight." It has an athletic flavor and is used of the spiritual "race" in Hebrews 12:1.

St. Paul here means that in his labors in the apostolic arena to win the prize (see 1 Cor. 9:24–27), he draws upon *God's* power, not his own. God's **working works in** him **with power.** The noun translated *working* (Gr. *energeia*), with its cognate verb *works* (Gr. *energeo*), is always in the New Testament used of supernatural power. St. Paul uses the word here to indicate the supernatural, miraculous energies of God, active in him in the power of the Holy Spirit. The glory of his apostolate does not belong therefore to him. It belongs to God, who works through him with His supernatural power.

§VI   Warning Against Gnostic Heresy (2:1—3:4)

ॐ ॐ ॐ ॐ ॐ

2 1   **For I want you to know how great a contest I have for you and for those in Laodicea, and for all those who have not seen my face in the flesh,**

2   **that their hearts may be encouraged, having been knit-together in love, for all the riches of the full-assurance of insight, for a real-knowledge of God's mystery,** *which is* **Christ,**

3   **in whom all the treasures of wisdom and knowledge are hidden.**

4   **I say this that no one will delude you with smooth-talk.**

Having described the cosmic Christ and His salvation, St. Paul comes at last to one of his main reasons for writing: to warn the Christians in the Lycus Valley of the heretical movement gaining popularity there. He **wants** them **to know** how much he is worried. That is, he thinks it important to reveal his inner heart to them, for his internal stress and **contest** for them is a sign of their danger. This **contest** (Gr. *agon*) is a reference to his striving in prayer for them (see 4:12, where he writes that their own Epaphras "contends [Gr. *agonizomai*] for them in his prayers"). The danger is so great that St. Paul's prayers for them are no casual mention. Rather, he agonizes for them (in our modern English sense of that word), with the striving of an athlete spending time and effort, pouring himself into his intercession, praying that **their hearts may be encouraged** and strengthened, that they might be **knit-together** and united in love for one another.

That is, he prays that they might have courage to stand alone for the Gospel in the world and that they might maintain the warm unity of mutual love in the face of schisms. It is only by having such spiritual maturity that they will be able to have all **the full-assurance of insight** of the truth (for we need each other to grow in Christ; see Eph. 3:17–19). The phrase *the full-assurance of insight* means the inner confidence that comes from discerning the truth from falsehood. Once they have matured, they can have the confidence in their Faith and the inner conviction that will allow them to resist the Gnostics. They will be able to see through their lies and not be rattled by their seductive **smooth-talk**. In this way, they will have **real-knowledge** [Gr. *epignosis*] **of . . . Christ**. That is, they will have intimate and true knowledge of the Lord. He is the true **mystery** of God—not the proffered fables of the Gnostics. The Gnostics claim that they possess the **hidden treasures of wisdom and knowledge**, the secret lore that will enable their elite to pass safely through the heavenly spheres. St. Paul counters that to know the Lord Jesus is enough, for all the **treasures of wisdom and knowledge** have been **hidden** in *Him*! To truly know Him is to know and possess all that God has for us.

৵৵ ৵৵ ৵৵ ৵৵ ৵৵

5   For though I am absent in the flesh, neverthe-
    less I am with you in the spirit, rejoicing and
    seeing your order and the solidity of your faith
    in Christ.

Finally, St. Paul assures them, the Christians of Colossae and Laodicea and others of the Lycus Valley whom he has not actually met **in the flesh**, that he is one with them and that they are important to him nonetheless. He is **with** them **in the spirit** and **rejoices** to see their **order** and discipline and **the solidity of** their **faith**. These words *order* and *solidity* have a military feel about them: *order* connotes men arrayed in their ranks and their proper places for battle, while *solidity* speaks of the immovable bulwarks of the army. Using these words, St. Paul seems like a general, inspecting the troops and **rejoicing** in their readiness for battle. He emphasizes his joy at the thought of their stability, for in this—in his love for them and his spiritual agony at the thought of their danger—is his moral authority to exhort them. He has never actually met them. They are Epaphras' spiritual children. His moral authority to teach them lies in the fact of his suffering for them (see 1:24). For it is only insofar as we love and suffer for others that we have the right to teach and direct them.

ॐ ॐ ॐ ॐ ॐ

6   Therefore as you have received the Christ, Jesus, the Lord, walk in Him,

7   having been rooted and being built-up in Him and confirmed in the Faith, just as you were taught, abounding in thanksgiving.

St. Paul begins his long warning against Gnostic teaching. He begins by referring them back to the original apostolic Tradition which they have **received**. For the word *received* (Gr. *paralambano*) is a technical word for receiving a tradition which has been delivered (see 1 Cor. 15:3, where St. Paul speaks of "delivering" the tradition that he himself also "received").

The Colossians have **received** the apostolic Tradition regarding **the Christ, Jesus, the Lord,** and they should continue to **walk** faithfully according to that, consistent with their original teaching. They were once-for-all **rooted** in this tradition through their baptismal catechesis and now are being continually **built-up** and **confirmed** by the ongoing homiletic teaching. (The verb *rooted* is in the perfect tense, denoting a completed past action—their catechismal instruction; whereas the verbs **built-up** and **confirmed** are in the present tense, denoting an ongoing present action—the homilies they are receiving from their clergy.) This is their experience, and St. Paul exhorts them not to swerve from the path they have taken. They are to continue to **walk** in it, **abounding in thanksgiving** (Gr. *eucharistia*)—not just during their Sunday Liturgies, but all the time. For rejoicing in the Lord and giving thanks for His salvation is the antidote for the Gnostic poison and will preserve them from the doubts the heretics would sow in their hearts.

༃ ༃ ༃ ༃ ༃

8   Watch out lest anyone capture you through philosophy and empty deceit, according to the tradition of men, according to the elements of the world, and not according to Christ,

9   for in Him all the fullness of the Godhead dwells bodily,

---

St. Paul continues to warn his hearers to **watch out** for the Gnostic threat lest they be **captured** by it. The word *capture* (Gr. *sulagogeo*) is the word used of a slave trader carrying off a vanquished foe to captivity, of a kind of kidnapping. The Gnostics would carry off the Colossians as plunder, taking them captive—not through force of arms, but through **philosophy and empty deceit**, through their pretended wisdom and useless lies. All of this smacks of **the tradition of men** and the **elements** (or rudimentary teachings) **of the world**. All this Gnostic theosophy—with its rules about circumcision and food laws and holy days—is just the same basic religious stuff, suited only for the immature, that you could get anywhere in the world. It is not **according to Christ**, in whom we have been brought beyond all this basic religion. This stuff pertains so obviously just to this age. In Christ, we have been "removed to the Kingdom" (see 1:13) and age to come and have left all this immaturity far behind.

The apostle says that they should not abandon the apostolic Christ for Gnostic counterfeits, for in Him they possess **all the fullness of the Godhead**. Christ is not just one link in the Fullness of the Godhead's series of emanations. All the Divine Fullness dwells in Him. And not only that, but the Divine Fullness dwells in Him **bodily** (Gr. *somatikos*). It is not, as the Gnostics asserted, that the true Divine Nature would not deign to soil Itself with contact with the bodily, corruptible world. On the contrary, the Fullness of God has actually assumed a body, sharing our physical nature.

ॐ ॐ ॐ ॐ ॐ

10 and in Him you have been fulfilled, and He is the Head of all rule and authority;

11 and in Him you were also circumcised with a circumcision made-without-hands, in the stripping-off of the body of the flesh in the circumcision of Christ;

12 having been co-buried with Him in Baptism, in which you were also co-raised with Him through faith in the working of God, who raised Him from the dead.

13 And you, who were dead in your offenses and the uncircumcision of your flesh, He co-quickened with Him, having forgiven us all our offenses,

---

Because Christ is the Fullness of Godhead, in possessing Him, we have been **fulfilled** and completed. As the apostle prayed for his Ephesian converts, our goal is to be "filled with all the fullness of God" and to reach the "stature of the fullness of Christ" (Eph. 3:19; 4:13). This is the true *theosis* and divinization, our final glorification in the Lord. When we are conformed to the image of Him who is the fullness of the Godhead, we will be **fulfilled** and complete indeed!

St. Paul continues with his description of the sufficiency of Christ for our salvation. It would seem that, in the Colossian form of Gnosticism with which the apostle was dealing, the concept of heavenly rulers and authorities was combined with the necessity of Jewish circumcision. Perhaps it had something to do with the thought that the Law was delivered by God to Israel through the hand of intermediary angels (see Acts 7:53). It could be that the Colossian Gnostics said that the way up through the heavenly spheres, guarded by heavenly rulers and authorities, would not be granted by them if one had disregarded the prescriptions of the Law which they had mediated. Thus, one needed to keep all the Jewish Law and give the proper homage and worship to these angelic guardians of the heavenly spheres if one were to gain access and safely reach the heavenly destination.

In opposition to these Gnostic assertions, St. Paul insists that Christ is all that is needed to be **fulfilled**, for He is **Head of all rule and authority**. He is the Head and King of all the angels, the Lord over all the heavenly spheres. If He opens the Kingdom to all believers, no other angelic ruler or authority has anything else to say. What He opens, no one can shut! Jewish circumcision also is entirely superfluous. Why seek this handmade and physical circumcision (see Eph. 2:11)? They have a better one—their baptism, the **circumcision of Christ**, one **made-without-hands**—i.e. one done supernaturally, by the Hand of God (see Dan. 2:45 for the concept of a work done "without hands"). Jewish circumcision removed only a small piece of flesh, but this baptismal **circumcision** removed and **stripped off** the whole **body of the flesh**, the entire old life, and left it behind (see Col. 3:9).

In baptism, they were incorporated into Christ and shared His death and Resurrection, being **co-buried** and **co-raised** with Him. Previously, they had been spiritually **dead** to God through their **offenses**; their life was one of **uncircumcision**. Through their fleshly ways, they were hostile to Him, with hard and uncircumcised hearts (see Deut. 10:16). Even so, through their baptism they came to share Christ's Resurrection life, being **co-quickened** with Him.

ॐ ॐ ॐ ॐ ॐ

14 having blotted-out the handwriting of decrees against us, which was adverse to us; and He

> has taken it out of the midst, having nailed it
> to the Cross.

All their offenses are now forgiven. The **handwriting** of their debt has been eliminated. Here St. Paul uses the image of a legal IOU. It is as if we signed in our own handwriting an agreement to keep the Law, and when we failed to do so, this became a certificate of debt, consisting of the Law's **decrees** which we had not kept. These were **adverse** to us (Gr. *upenantion*; see its use in Heb. 10:27 for the "adversaries" of God)—they were hostile and our enemy. This debt and IOU Christ **blotted-out,** absolutely wiping it out as ink is washed off the page. He also **took it out of the midst,** setting it entirely to one side, banishing it from our life. He did this through His death, **nailing** the IOU (as it were) **to the Cross.** Here we have a defiant and ironic image (of the kind in which Orthodoxy has always delighted). The Cross seemed to the world to be the defeat of Christ. On the contrary, asserts St. Paul, it was His victory! What was **nailed to the Cross** and killed in defeat was not the Lord, but the certificate of our debt and guilt! Just as the accusation against Christ was fastened over His Head (Matt. 27:37), so the accusations against us were fastened to His Cross and forever removed from us.

> ॐ ॐ ॐ ॐ ॐ
>
> 15 Having stripped-off the rulers and authorities,
> He disgraced them openly, having led them as
> triumphal captives through it.

The Cross was not the **disgrace** and public shame of the Lord. What was openly disgraced was the enemy, the demonic **rulers and authorities,** when our Lord **stripped** them **off** through His death, like a mighty conqueror stripping his captives of their armor and weapons. Just as a conqueror led his vanquished foes in procession as captives, to their public disgrace, so the Lord by His Cross led these fallen angels as captives in His triumphal train. The Cross was not the Lord's disgraceful defeat. As the kontakion of the Feast of the Elevation of the Cross says, it was His triumph, "the invincible trophy, the weapon of peace." Through all of these images St. Paul showed how Christ was all that was needed for complete forgiveness and salvation. Placation of heavenly powers by keeping of the Jewish Law was entirely superfluous and useless. The Cross and Resurrection of Christ was sufficient for all.

---

16 Therefore let no one judge you regarding food or drink or about a feast or a new moon or Sabbaths—

17 things which are a shadow of things to come; but the body is of Christ.

18 Let no one disqualify you, insisting in humble-mindedness and the worshipping of the angels, taking his stand on what he has seen, vainly puffed up by the mind of his flesh,

19 and not holding fast to the Head, from whom all the Body, being supplied and knit-together by the joints and bonds, grows with the growth of God.

The Gnostics were trying to intimidate the Colossians by judging them for not keeping the Law. Without keeping the Law, they said, there could be no salvation. To this St. Paul answers that the Colossians have nothing to fear for not keeping Jewish dietary laws or Jewish feasts and holy days and Sabbaths. These things are but the **shadow** and prefiguring of the substantial truth which is to come. The **body** (Gr. *soma*) or substance belongs to Christ. He is what all these Jewish prefigurings are leading to. They are the prophecy; He is the solid reality. Thus the Colossians should not let these heretics **disqualify** them. The word in Greek is *katabrabeuo*, which literally means "to rule as empire against them." The image is of an empire or judge giving a disqualifying judgment and thus robbing them of their victory. The Gnostics, by perverting the faith of the Colossians, would take their prize from them. In more idiomatic and colloquial English, St. Paul tells them, "Don't let anyone rip you off!"

This was a very necessary warning, for the Gnostics could appear very persuasive and attractive. They **insisted in humblemindedness** (Gr. *thelon en tapeinophrosune*, literally, "willing in humblemindedness," apparently a Semitism). That is, they gave a great and elaborate show of humility, as befitting incredibly spiritual persons who had seen great angelic visions. It would seem that the propagators of this Gnostic heresy asserted that they had been initiated into awesome and higher mystic realities. They had contact with the **angels**, the guardians of the heavenly spheres—to whom proper homage and **worship** (Gr. *threskeia* or religious cult) must be given in order to pass through the heavens. This was what they asserted (it would seem), and it was a very potent and persuasive mix of pretended piety and advanced esoterica. They put on airs that they were so much more spiritually privileged than the poor uninitiated followers of St. Paul and Epaphras, as they **took** their **stand** on their mystic experiences. The word translated *taking his stand* (Gr. *embateuo*) is the technical term for treading upon sacred ground by some initiated person. In St. Paul's usage here, it refers to the Gnostic's boast that he has entered upon a higher state of being as a result of the visions and illuminations that he has allegedly **seen**.

St. Paul warns the Colossians not to be impressed by this spurious show of spirituality. In reality, these people are **vainly puffed up by the mind of** their **flesh**. They are not truly spiritual at all, but fleshly and conceited, with their mind and orientation bounded by things of the world. They are not **holding fast** to Christ, the **Head** of His Body the Church. As such, they are not **supplied** (as the Colossians are) with the grace of God through relationships in the Church (see Eph. 4:16) and do not **grow with the growth** and life **of God**. Though they claim to be mature and advanced, they are actually cut off and deprived of true spiritual life.

ॐ ॐ ॐ ॐ ॐ

20 If you have died with Christ to the elements of the world, why, as if living in the world, do you submit-to-decrees, *like*
21 "Do not handle, do not taste, do not touch!"
22 (which *things* all *go* to corruption *as they are* used-up)—in accordance with the injunctions and teachings of men?—
23 which things indeed have a report of wisdom in self-made-religion and humblemindedness and severity to the body, but are of no value for *stopping* gratification of the flesh.

As the answer to such pretensions, the apostle once again refers to their baptism (see v. 12), reminding them that in baptism they **died with Christ** (see Rom. 6:3–8) to this age. They have transcended this age with all its religious categories, **elements,** and rudimentary values. They no longer have their life in this **world,** but have been removed and transplanted to the age to come (see 1:13). Thus it makes no sense to **submit-to-decrees** of the Law such as **"Do not handle, do not taste, do not touch!"** for these are clearly decrees of this age, and not the realities of the age to come in which they now live. (These decrees and prohibitions seem to have been a Gnostic appropriation of the Jewish Law, reinterpreted according to Gnosticism's own peculiar rigor. For the dietary laws of Judaism do not seem to have forbidden touching of forbidden foods, but the Gnostic rigorism here envisioned seems to have proscribed *any* contact with forbidden food—"Do not even *touch* it!")

The nature of the **decrees** makes clear the worldly and transitory nature of the religion which issues them. For these **decrees** have to do with such things as food—which perish in **corruption** as they are **used-up.** That is, as soon as it is put to use, it ceases to be. This in itself shows that this Gnostic religion does not have to do with eternal realities, but merely with the things of this transitory and passing age. It is not a divine religion, but merely another one of the all-too-human religions and **teachings of men**.

Admittedly, these things have a **report** or appearance (Gr. *logos*) **of wisdom**. They exult in **self-made-religion** (Gr. *ethelothreskia*)— that is, in a kind of do-it-yourself, make-it-up-as-you-go religion. It delights to show off how spiritual it is, with its fake **humble-mindedness** and its **severity to the body**, its superficial and false asceticism. All of these things are mere window-dressing. They are self-consciously designed to show off how spiritual it all is, but they are, after all, of **no value** in stopping true and inner fleshly **gratification**. For they have their origin in the flesh—it is to gratify the fleshly desire to boast and to appear superior that these things were invented in the first place. It is all so obviously of this earth.

---

꣓ ꣓ ꣓ ꣓ ꣓

3 1 **Therefore if you have been co-raised with the Christ, seek the things above, where the Christ is, seated at the right hand of God.**

2 **Mind the things above, not the things on the earth.**

3 **For you have died and your life has been hidden with the Christ in God.**

4 **When Christ, who is our life, is manifested, then you also will be manifested with Him in glory.**

In baptism, however, the Colossians were **co-raised with the Christ** and now live with Him. (We note in passing that, in these verses, the definite article is used four times: not just "Christ," but **the Christ**, in order to stress the dignity of Jesus as the glorified Messiah.) Thus, as living in the heavenly Christ, they should leave behind all these **things on the earth** and seek instead **the things above, where the Christ is, seated at the right hand of God.**

The reference here is not to things that are sinful (though they should not seek those either!). Rather, the reference is to the earthly concerns of the Gnostic religion—things such as dietary laws and other prohibitions of the Jewish Law. Their **mind**, attitude, and orientation should no longer be on such earthly concerns. In baptism, they were incorporated into Christ. Their true life is now in Him, and since He is now **seated at the right hand of God**, their thoughts must be on heavenly and eternal realities also. They **died** with Christ to this age. They are now altogether heavenly and belong to the age to come. Their true life is **hidden . . . in God**, in heaven, safe from all the changes and chances of this world. Thus, when Christ is **manifested** at the Second Coming, they will be **manifested in glory** along with Him, for they are in Him.

Note here the close and indissoluble link between Christ and His members that baptism establishes. Baptism incorporates us into Christ so that all that He is, we are also. Christ died and so we die. Christ was raised and we are co-raised with Him. Christ sits at the right hand of God and, in Him, so do we. This is the true and final answer to Gnosticism with its earthly categories and claims. Christ is above all these worldly concerns and therefore, we are too. Since we are in Him through our baptism, we share His heavenly transcendence and are above all the passing things of earth. However attractive Gnosticism may appear, it is ultimately below us.

St. Paul's denunciation of Gnosticism as it presented itself to the Christians of the Lycus Valley has a lasting value for us today. That exact form of Gnosticism may not have survived to our day, but its spiritual descendants are still with us. The many forms of theosophy, anthroposophy, and other variations of New Age spirituality still offer a potent and heady mix to those seeking a spirituality more exotic than what they think they know as the traditional Christian Faith. The lure of the unfamiliar, combined with exalted claims to provide mystic illumination, can be intensely attractive to those seeking something new and exciting. The Church will always have to contend with those who falsely claim to offer a more "spiritual" approach. And its answer will always be the same—to reveal the ultimately earthbound nature of such "spiritualities" and our transcendence of them through our union with Christ.

§VII   Exhortation to Holiness (3:5—4:1)

§VII.1 Putting off the old life (3:5–11)

ॐ ॐ ॐ ॐ ॐ

5   Therefore put to death the members which are on the earth—fornication, uncleanness, passion, evil desire, and greed, which is idolatry.

6   For it is because of these things that the wrath of God will come,

7   and in them you also once walked, when you lived in them.

Having warned them against negative and false teaching, St. Paul goes on to exhort them to positive holiness. Because they have been raised with Christ and are in Him in the heavenlies (v. 3), **therefore** they should **put to death** their **members which are on the earth**. They are now of the heavens, while such sinful behavior as they worked in the past with their **members** belonged to their old earthly life. (Thus St. Paul describes their sins as done with their **members which are on the earth**—for these acts were done before they were raised up to heaven with Christ and began seeking the things above.)

The word translated *put to death* is in the aorist tense, indicating that they should once-for-all reckon themselves as dead to sinful behavior, making a decisive and absolute break with it. The verb here is also different from that used in Romans 8:13. There St. Paul tells them to "put to death" their sins (Gr. *thanatoo*)—meaning "to slay, execute." Here the word *put to death* (Gr. *nekroo*) has a flavor of killing by wearing out. It is used of the worn-out, impotent body of Abraham, whose body was as good as "having been put to death" (Rom. 4:19; Heb. 11:12). Here in Colossians, there is the nuance of not putting any energy, any life, into these forms of behavior. These sins die of neglect!

The sins that St. Paul singles out for mention are the sins of **fornication** (Gr. *porneia*), which was all but universal in the pagan world; **uncleanness** (Gr. *akatharsia*), meaning any form of sexual sin (such as pornography, for example); **passion** (Gr. *pathos*), meaning any overwhelming, consuming compulsion (not necessarily sexual); **evil desire** (Gr. *epithumian kaken*), indicating appetites and insatiable craving for evil things; and finally **greed** (Gr. *pleonexia*). This last is equated with **idolatry**, since to be ruled by greed is to make an idol of the thing desired. Our hearts are to find rest and satisfaction in God alone; to be totally consumed with a desire for anything else (so that we can have no rest until we possess it) is to make of that thing our true god. Thus St. Paul says that the greedy man is really an idolater, for he has given his heart over to something other than the living God.

In singling out these sins, St. Paul would paint a picture of the pagan world in which the Colossian Christians once lived. It is this very lifestyle, these very sins, which will one day bring the wrath of God upon the world on the Last Day. If they would avoid this final wrath, they must now shun this culture of death. They *used* to **live** this way, **walking** in these sins. Their whole life was steeped and stained by them. But no more: now they have a new life—one "hidden with the Christ in God" (v. 3). There can be no going back. St. Paul stresses here that these things belong to their past— and they must now let the past be past. There is no place for these things in their present life now.

ॐ ॐ ॐ ॐ ॐ

8 But now you *yourselves* also, put them all off: wrath, indignation, malice, reviling, and obscenity from your mouth.

St. Paul goes on to further separate them from the old ways. Not only the obvious sins such as fornication, but *every* bit of the old man and old life must go. Even sins such as anger in all its sinful forms must be laid aside: **wrath** (Gr. *orge*) or habitual anger; **indignation** (Gr. *thumos*) or explosions of sudden fury; **malice** (Gr. *kakia*) or bad feeling, cherished ill will which broods over insults and injustices, real or imagined; **reviling** (Gr. *blasphemia*) or cutting verbal abuse and insult; and finally **obscenity** (Gr. *aischrologia*) or foul-mouthed swearing. All of these kinds of talk must no longer come **from** their **mouths** but must be once-and-for-all **put off** (even as they put off their old garments in preparation for baptism). The mouths which now offer eucharistic praise to God must not utter such horrible things (see James 3:9, 10).

৵৽ ৵৽ ৵৽ ৵৽ ৵৽

9   Do not lie to one another, since you stripped off the old man with his practices,

10 and have put on the new *man* who is being renewed to a real-knowledge according to *the* image of *Him* who created him—

11 where there is no Greek and Jew, circumcision and uncircumcision, barbarian, Scythian, slave *or* freeman, but Christ is all, and in all.

They must live in harmony, not **lying** to one another, using one another, telling falsehoods to get what they want. This was part of the **old man** and former life, with all its nefarious **practices** and false ways, which were **stripped off** in baptism. Through that sacramental Mystery they **put on** the new self (even as they put on garments after their baptism). Through this they were continually and progressively being **renewed** (Gr. *anakainoo*). The root word in Greek for this renewal is the word *kainos*—"new" in the sense of "brand-new, fresh, unused."

Our baptismal renewal is thus the ongoing restoration of the freshness of our original creation. It is through this that we come to an intimate **real-knowledge** (Gr. *epignosis*) of our Creator. St. Paul says here that we were originally created in God's **image** to know Him and share His joy. Sin obscured this image and ruined this fellowship, but now, through Christ, this image is being restored so that we can walk with God and know Him once again. In this baptismal renewal, we have all **put on the new *man*.**

In this new creation all earthly categories and divisions have been transcended. People of all kinds are equally given this new life. Thus in this new creation there are no longer any racial divisions, such as **Greek and Jew**. Even religious divisions (such as **circumcision and uncircumcision**) are no more. Cultural barriers too are abolished—the uncultured non-Greek **barbarian** is given new life, alongside his cultured Greek-speaking comrade. Even the **Scythians**—thought to be the lowest of the low, the most barbarous of the barbarians—can be received on equal terms.

And—most outrageous in the ancient world—the differences between the **slave** and **freeman** are transcended. This was perhaps most shocking of all, for the ancients (such as Aristotle for example) considered a slave to be but a living tool, not different in kind from any other inanimate object. That even slaves were to be given the same new life and salvation as their free masters was revolutionary. It was the crowning sign that this renewal and baptismal new creation was something utterly new in the earth. Absolutely all social divisions have been swept away. The only abiding reality is Christ— He **is all** and everything and the only thing that matters. And He is **in all**. He is in everyone in the Church, without regard for their former race, religion, culture, or social position. If Christ is thus in every one of their Christian brothers and sisters, how can they possibly treat them badly, lying to them, using them? To do so would be to sin against Christ.

§VII.2 Putting on the new life (3:12–17)

3⅋ 3⅋ 3⅋ 3⅋ 3⅋

12 Put on therefore, as chosen of God, holy and beloved, compassionate heartfelt *love*, kindness, humblemindedness, meekness, and patience;

13 bearing with one another, and forgiving each other, whoever has a complaint against anyone; as the Lord forgave you, thus you *yourselves should do* also.

The **therefore** refers to the prior declaration of Christ being all in all. Since Christ is "in all," they must honor and love one another. As they "stripped off" the old life at their baptism, so they must **put on** the life of the new creation, even as they put on their garments after their baptismal immersion. More specifically, as God's **chosen** people, the new Israel (see Eph. 2:12), they must **put on** the virtues befitting their new life and status.

Formerly they were on a collision course with "the wrath of God" (v. 6). Now they are **holy and beloved**, objects of God's care and protection, and they must strive to live worthy of their calling. They should manifest **compassionate heartfelt** *love* (Gr. *splagchna oiktirmou*—literally "bowels of compassion," for the bowels were considered the seat of yearning). That is, they should yearn and care for one another with true compassion and concern. Also, they should manifest **kindness, humblemindedness, meekness, and patience.** In their life together as a holy and beloved community, they should take care to be gentle with one another, not boasting and competing, but seeking to serve. They should control their impulses and tame their tongues and always "give the other person space," "cutting them slack." As God bears with them, forgiving them and never despairing of them (see the Lord's forbearance in Matt. 17:17), so they must do for one another. For as a community, they would all have a just **complaint** against each other, as they hurt and wound one another. It would be easy to despair and to build walls for their own protection. This is just what is forbidden. They are to remain open and vulnerable to each other, no matter what the cost. Thus the Lord remained vulnerable to us, though it led (as it must) to the Cross. It was from the Cross that He forgave us, and we must do the same.

***

14 Above all these things, *add* love, which is the bond of perfection.

The crown and completion of all their striving to live together as the holy chosen people is **love**. This is the **bond of perfection**, the holy chain that binds them all together into spiritual maturity and completeness. If they have this, they have all that they need. This **love** (Gr. *agape*) is not a mere warm feeling toward the other, for feelings come and go and cannot be summoned. Rather, it is the steely determination to serve the other, seeking his salvation and joy, no matter what the personal cost; the persevering action of meeting the other's need, of seeing her as God sees her. Love therefore is detached, in that the loving person will not be entangled in his own hurts and needs, but will shake himself free to serve the other relentlessly.

ॐ ॐ ॐ ॐ ॐ

15 Let the peace of Christ rule-as-empire in your hearts, to which indeed you were called in one Body; and be thankful.

The word translated **rule-as-empire** is *brabeueto*; it is sometimes translated "act as arbiter" or "control." The concept is one of giving a ruling. What St. Paul means here is that the presence (or absence) of the **peace of Christ** in their hearts should be the judge of their actions—whatever preserves this peace may be judged as good, and whatever causes His peace to depart from their hearts may be judged as wrong. For they are **called** to this peace **in one Body**. That is, unity and **peace** constitute the essential nature of the Kingdom. The sinful and rebellious world is characterized by chaos, warfare, and mutual hostility. In the Kingdom, the original cosmic harmony is restored, and it is to this that they are all **called** in **one** and the same **Body** through their baptism. Thus, the presence of Christ's peace is the sure and dependable sign that their actions are good and are manifestations of the Kingdom. They are to preserve this harmony and peace and **be thankful** (Gr. *eucharistos*). That is, they are to let the eucharistic unity and gratitude of their Sunday

Liturgies spill over into the week and thus live lives of peace and thanksgiving.

ॐ ॐ ॐ ॐ ॐ

16 Let the Word of Christ dwell in you richly, with all wisdom teaching and admonishing one another with psalms and hymns and spiritual songs, singing with grace in your hearts to God.

The **Word of Christ** is the teaching found in the Church, the homiletic and instructive word that inspires them to live worthy of the Lord. They are exhorted to let this Word **dwell richly** in them— that is, they are to let this teaching find a home in their hearts, and an abundant and rich welcome among them. The collective community is to be receptive to the divine message. Their singing is to be a mirror and response to the Gospel teaching; they are to **teach and admonish one another** as they sing their **psalms** (the Psalter), their **hymns** (original Church compositions), and their **spiritual songs** (singing in prophecy; see 1 Cor. 14:15). Thus their liturgical praise is not merely addressed to the Lord. It is also of benefit to themselves, as they rehearse the Word of Christ **with all wisdom, singing with grace** (Gr. *en chariti*) in their hearts. For the Word of Christ which pours from their lips bubbles up from the divine grace in their hearts and causes that grace itself to multiply and abound. The Church's liturgical song is thus itself an instrument of God, by which He teaches and transforms His people.

ॐ ॐ ॐ ॐ ॐ

17 And whatever you do in word or work, do all in the Name of the Lord Jesus, giving thanks to God the Father through Him.

The goal of all their life and liturgy together is to do all in the Lord's Name. That is, they are to manifest the Lord's life on earth, as His Body. To do something **in the Name of the Lord Jesus** means to do it as His representative, on His authority and as the manifestation of His life. The Colossians are thus not to live for themselves. Rather, as St. Paul says elsewhere, it should no longer be they who live, but Christ who lives in them (see Gal. 2:20). Their life is His life. Their existence is to be one continuous outpouring of thanksgiving (Gr. *eucharisteo*) to God in His Name. The Christian calling is to be a eucharistic man.

§VII.3 Living together in family (3:18—4:1)

ৡৡ ৡৡ ৡৡ ৡৡ ৡৡ

18 Wives, submit to the husbands, as is fitting in *the* Lord.

19 Husbands, love the wives and do not be embittered against them.

20 Children, obey the parents in all things, for this is well-pleasing in *the* Lord.

21 Fathers, do not provoke your children, so that they will not be discouraged.

22 Slaves, in all things obey your lords according to the flesh, not with eye-service, as men-pleasers, but in singleness of heart, fearing the Lord.

23 Whatever you do, work from the soul, as to the Lord rather than to men,

24 knowing that from the Lord you will receive the recompense of the inheritance. It is the Lord Christ whom you *serve as* slaves.

25 For he who does wrong will receive-back the wrong which he has done, and there is no respect of persons.

4 1 Lords, present to your slaves that which is just and equal, knowing that you too have a Lord in heaven.

St. Paul concludes his exhortations to holiness by a brief series of directives to the various groups in the Christian household. **Wives** are to **submit** to their husbands—not with any cringing servility, but with a respectful love. In this way, society at large will see the Christian Faith is not the dangerous, fanatical thing it was popularly slandered as being (see Titus 2:4, 5). This submission is **fitting in *the* Lord**—that is, it is the way they can adorn and express their discipleship to Christ, for the Lord taught and embodied lowliness of heart and true humility, as He Himself submitted to His Father. **Husbands** for their part are to **love** their wives and **not be embittered** against them. That is, even if their wives are not submissive and sweet-spirited, the husbands must not react with bitterness and recrimination. They must continue to **love** them and return good for evil, responding with never-failing gentleness to any nagging, insult, or complaint.

Children are to **obey** their **parents** in everything (assuming of course that they are yet minors living with them at home). This refusal to disobey and rebel is **well-pleasing in *the* Lord** and thus will bring His blessing on them as they grow. **Fathers** (to whom was entrusted the discipline of the children) are not to **provoke** their children, lest they become discouraged. The word translated *provoke* (Gr. *erethizo*) means "to arouse," either for good or ill (see 2 Cor. 9:2 for arousing in a good way). Here it clearly means to drive to distraction, to break the child's spirit by excessive severity. This is not how our heavenly Father deals with us. Earthly fathers must imitate the gentleness and patience of God with their children.

The directive to **slaves** is four times the length of each of the other directives. It is here that St. Paul feels the most exhortation is needed, perhaps because slaves constitute so much of the Christian community there. Certainly bad behavior from the Christian slaves could bring the Faith into serious disrepute. The apostle's concern here is for them to "adorn the teaching" in the sight of men and give it credibility by their actions (see Titus 2:10). The **slaves** therefore are to serve their earthly lords with true service, from their very **soul** and inner heart. They should work hard, not just when they are being watched (with **eye-service as men-pleasers**). For they do not belong ultimately to men, but to their true Lord and Master, the **Lord Christ**, and He will recompense them on the Last Day for their work (whether noticed by men or not), giving them their imperishable **inheritance** (see Rom. 8:17). Similarly, any wrongdoing, insubordination, or pilfering will be judged. There is no partiality, no **respect of persons**. They should not expect to be exempt from judgment simply because they are Christians and their masters are not.

The earthly **lords** and masters are not to tyrannize over their slaves. They are to offer their slaves justice and fairness, not dealing with a favored one leniently and a less favored one more severely. For these earthly **lords** also have a divine **Lord in heaven**, and He will judge any high-handed favoritism.

In this discussion of slavery, it must be understood that St. Paul is not laying down a blueprint for a Christian secular society. Rather, he is writing instructions for life in society as he found it. Slavery was indeed incompatible with the Gospel, for the Gospel affirmed that slaves were not mere "living tools" (as the pagans said), but children of God. When the Gospel leaven had leavened society, slavery did indeed at length shrivel and die. But St. Paul's concern here is not for such long-range plans. It is for the Christians of the Lycus Valley in his day and for how they can live as the disciples of Jesus in the midst of their pagan society.

§VIII Final Admonitions (4:2–6)

St. Paul finishes his epistle with a few brief admonitions. These cannot be considered unimportant trifles, merely tacked on at the end as a careless afterthought. On the contrary, they have a great significance, for it is these things that the apostle would leave ringing in their ears as they conclude his letter. (Thus they are parallel to the concluding admonition to "put on the panoply of God" in the "companion epistle" to the Ephesians [Eph. 6:10–17].)

> ॐ ॐ ॐ ॐ ॐ
>
> 2   Be devoted to prayer, being alert in it with thanksgiving;

These admonitions are peculiarly suited to living as a Christian in a hostile environment. Indeed, St. Paul, sitting in a Roman prison while he writes this, has great experience of that hostility! Of first importance in such an environment is that they be **devoted to prayer**. It is this lifeline to the Divine which will preserve them and give them strength for the battle. The reference is primarily to private domestic prayer at home (Sunday corporate worship is presupposed). The verb *be devoted* (Gr. *proskartereo*) means "to attach oneself to, to wait on someone, to be busily engaged." It means more here than merely persevering in prayer and not neglecting to say one's daily Rule. It means that prayer should be one's main or most important occupation, so that we give prayer as much time as we possibly can. Spare moments of the day should not be frittered away uselessly, but given over to prayer. (The Jesus Prayer, as an especially "portable" prayer, is wonderfully suited for just this purpose.) In our prayer, we are to **be alert**, watching, maintaining an inner spiritual vigilance. In their intercession, they are to watch for impending dangers (such as persecution), so that they are not blindsided and shaken in their faith (see 1 Pet. 5:8). Yet their prayer is not to be the frantic outpouring of the frightened. Rather, their alert prayers are to be offered **with thanksgiving** (Gr. *eucharistia*). God Most High is to be praised for His mercy and loving providential care, which is over all His works. For nothing can strike them or occur but such as God has allowed.

ॐ ॐ ॐ ॐ ॐ

3   praying together also for us, that God will open up to us a door for the Word, so that we may speak the mystery of the Christ, for which I have also been bound;

4   that I may make it manifest as I ought to speak.

Typically, St. Paul adds a humble request that they **pray together** for him (and his companions with him). Again typically, he does not ask that they pray for his acquittal and release. Rather, though sitting on trial for life, his only concern is for the advancement of the Faith. His desire is that **God will open up to us a door for the Word** of the Gospel. By **door** he means "opportunity" (see 1 Cor. 16:9; 2 Cor. 2:12). The opportunity he so covets is that of speaking to the great Caesar of **the mystery of the Christ**, long hidden from the world but now revealed through the apostles. It is for this very task that he has been **bound** in prison in the first place. He fears that the trial may revolve only around such political questions as his loyalty to the Roman state (see Acts 26:31, 32), when what he really wants is to use his audience with Caesar to preach Christ to him. This is the **door** that he wants God to open, so that he may **manifest** the Gospel boldly and effectively, as he **ought**.

ॐ ॐ ॐ ॐ ॐ

5   Walk in wisdom toward outsiders, redeeming the time.
6   Let your word always *be* with grace, as though seasoned with salt, so that you will know how you should answer each person.

As well as enjoining devotion to prayer, he tells the Colossians to **walk** and conduct themselves in true godliness and **wisdom** before the **outsiders**. Once again, **wisdom** is not the worldly shrewdness valued in the secular world, but insight into the hidden ways of God and of His true nature. They are to **walk** in imitation of their heavenly Father (see Eph. 5:1). In this way the world outside the Church can see the truth of the Gospel and know that the slanderous lies told about the Christians are untrue. And such slanders abounded! (When St. Paul first reached Rome, for example, he was informed by his Jewish compatriots that his "sect" was "spoken against everywhere" [Acts 28:22].) Those were days of stress for Christians, and thus it was important to **redeem the time**, buying up every opportunity to promote the Faith by good works and by walking wisely.

We note too that here St. Paul draws the decisive line (the one separating "insiders" from outsiders) as the boundaries of the Church. This reveals that the fundamental loyalty of those professing the Christian Faith is loyalty to their brothers and sisters in the Church. There may be other subordinate loyalties in our lives—loyalties and relationships based on politics, interests, service organizations, and family ties. These are important too, but are less significant and fundamental than our solidarity in Christ. All others in our lives, even the closest and dearest, if they do not share Jesus Christ, are ultimately **outsiders**. This is a hard saying, no doubt, but it is basic to our Faith. "If anyone comes to Me," the Lord said, "and does not hate his own father and mother and wife and children and brothers and sisters, yes, and even his own life, he cannot be My disciple" (Luke 14:26). Baptism thus decisively separates us from the world, making all outsiders to us. That is why the world experiences the Church as something alien in its midst: our ultimate loyalty is no longer there. Our hearts now belong to Jesus.

Because of this challenge of living in the world, St. Paul tells the Colossians to let their speech be **with grace, as though seasoned with salt**. Salt was, of course, the main preservative of the ancient world. Without it, things would rot and putrefy. St. Paul tells them, in effect, to keep their speech pure, to "let no corrupt or rotten word proceed from your mouth" so that their words will "give grace to those who hear" (Eph. 5:29). They should not thoughtlessly rattle on, speaking whatever comes into their heads. They should rather consider their words first, weighing them before they speak them, so that **each person** will be given the appropriate and fitting **answer**. The context here is dialogue with the outsiders, with those requiring an **answer** (though no doubt our speech among ourselves should be no less "graceful"!). The **grace** that **seasons** our speech has a flavor of wit (see the Latin expression "Attic salt," meaning "Attic wit"). This cultural nuance indicates that Christian responses are no dull, insipid, and humorless pieties. That type of all-too-common self-righteous response to the challenges and sins of the world does nothing to commend Christ to those who need Him! Rather, our words should have the wit of those fully alive and the tang of truth.

§IX   Final Personal News and Greetings (4:7–17)

ॐ ॐ ॐ ॐ ॐ

7   All the things concerning me, Tychicus, the beloved brother and faithful servant and fellow-slave in the Lord, will make known to you,

8   whom I have sent to you for this very thing, that you may know the things concerning me and that he may comfort your hearts;

9   *and* with *him* Onesimus, the faithful and beloved brother, who is *one* of you. All things here they will make known to you.

As is usual in letters in the ancient world, St. Paul concludes his epistle with final personal news and greetings. He begins by commending to them **Tychicus**, the bearer of the letter. He was sent for the very purpose of not only delivering the Colossian correspondence, but also personally passing on news of all **the things concerning** St. Paul so that **he may comfort** their **hearts**. (He also bears an epistle to the neighboring church of the Ephesians, as a kind of circular letter to the churches of Asia; see Eph. 6:21.) Accompanying him is **Onesimus**, the slave who ran away from Philemon's household in Colossae. He was converted while in Rome through the influence of St. Paul and is now being sent back home to face the music and be reconciled to his old master. (Tychicus has a special letter for Philemon as well, to help smooth the way home for Onesimus.) With his customary diplomacy, St. Paul refers to Onesimus the runaway slave in the same terms as the free man Tychicus, calling them both his **beloved brothers**. Note that Tychicus is also called the apostle's **fellow-slave**, whereas St. Paul, with a touch of subtle delicacy, does not make any reference to slavery (however metaphorical) when referring to the runaway Onesimus. Instead, he refers to him as **faithful**—a subtle commendation, aimed at those who thought the runaway slave rather obviously faithless. The only reference to his (notorious) past is the vague and general description that he is *one* of them. The presence of Onesimus, back home and accompanying Tychicus, would doubtless be very awkward initially for all involved. St. Paul shows his genius for loving sensitivity in the way he commends these two bearers of his correspondence—and especially in the way he groups them together, the slave and the free man, as one, as **they** who will **make known** to the Colossians all the news about St. Paul. To welcome Tychicus is also to welcome his companion, Onesimus.

ॐ ॐ ॐ ॐ ॐ

10 Aristarchus, my fellow-captive, greets you; and also Mark the cousin of Barnabas (concerning whom you received commandments; if he comes to you, welcome him);

He continues his personal news by sending the greetings of those who remain with him in Rome. Greetings are sent by **Aristarchus**, described by St. Paul with gentle humor as his **fellow-captive** (or fellow "prisoner of war"), since he voluntarily stayed with him during his imprisonment, working as his liaison to the outside. Aristarchus was with St. Paul in Ephesus and was himself almost lynched by an angry pagan mob when the silversmiths rose up to protest on behalf of "Artemis of the Ephesians" (Acts 19:28, 29). He was with the apostle when he departed for Rome, staying with him and sharing his hardship (Acts 27:2). He was a devoted fellow-laborer and a good man to have in a tight spot.

Also sending greetings was **Mark the cousin of Barnabas**. The subject of Mark was something of a delicate and awkward matter for St. Paul. Mark had accompanied Paul and Barnabas on an earlier apostolic journey, but had given up midway through and gone home. St. Paul then refused to take him along on their next journey, fearing that he would "leave them in the lurch" again. Barnabas violently disagreed, siding with his cousin and quarreling with Paul. The two had to agree to disagree: Barnabas took Mark with him and Paul took Silas instead (Acts 15:36–41). Now, however, they have patched up the quarrel. The Colossians have received **com-mandments** and instructions about Mark—possibly news about his intended itinerary from St. Paul himself. Here he tells them to **welcome** him if he comes. (We note in passing how the apostle does not dwell on the past. He does not blame Mark or go on about how much he has changed. He wastes no energy or time on it at all. The past is over: what matters now is the urgent duty of the present.)

ॐ ॐ ॐ ॐ ॐ

11 and Jesus (the one called Justus); these are the only co-workers for the Kingdom of God who are of the circumcision, and they have become a comfort to me.

Last to send greetings as one of St. Paul's Jewish compatriots is **Jesus (the one called Justus)**. His Hebrew name is Yeshua (or Joshua), the same name as the Lord's and also rendered in Greek as **Jesus**. As well as the Hebrew name Yeshua/Jesus, he also had another name, used when he traveled in Gentile circles—the name **Justus**. (This phenomenon of a double name was not unknown. The apostle himself seems to have rendered his Hebrew name Saul as Paul when among Gentile company. Even today, for example, many a Greek Demetrios will render his name as Jim among English-speaking society, based on an initial aural similarity.) Little else is known of this Jesus. He is not mentioned in the companion letter to Philemon. Perhaps, as a local Roman resident and visitor of St. Paul, he just happened to be with him at the time Paul dictated his letter to the Colossians and asked that the apostle add a greeting from him too. St. Paul is grateful for his **comfort** and commends him along with the others as a **co-worker for the Kingdom of God**.

ॐ ॐ ॐ ॐ ॐ

12 Epaphras, who is one of you, a slave of Jesus Christ, greets you, always contesting for you

> in his prayers, that you may stand perfect and
> fully-assured in all the will of God.
> 13 For I witness for him that he has much zeal for
> you and for those in Laodicea and Hierapolis.

St. Paul also passes along the greetings of their own beloved founder, **Epaphras**. He says that he **contests for** them **in his prayers** that they might finally **stand perfect and fully-assured in all the will of God**—that is, that they might reach true spiritual maturity and know to carry out all that God wills. The word translated (rather awkwardly) *contests* is the Greek *agonizomai*, cognate with the word *agon*, "athletic contest" or race (see its use in Heb. 12:1). Here it means that Epaphras labors mightily in his prayers for them, expending the sweat and effort of an athlete in his contest, striving with all his might. It is the measure of his love and concern for his spiritual children, for whom he has **much zeal** and deep concern—not only those in Colossae, but also those in neighboring **Laodicea and Hierapolis**.

> ৵৽ ৵৽ ৵৽ ৵৽ ৵৽
>
> 14 Luke, the beloved physician, and Demas greet
> you.

Also passing on greetings is **Luke, the beloved physician**. Luke was the apostle's companion for much of his apostolic journey. As a healer of the heart as well as the body, he stayed with St. Paul with true selfless devotion. At the end of the apostle's life, when awaiting execution at the end of his second imprisonment, he could declare, "Only Luke is with me" (2 Tim. 4:11). Like a dedicated physician waiting on his sick patient through the lonely hours of the long night, Luke stayed with his apostolic friend through thick and thin.

Last to send greetings was **Demas**. Not much else is said of him, simply the name. This is perhaps significant. At the end of the apostle's life, he says that Demas had deserted him for Thessalonica, "having loved the present age" (2 Tim. 4:10). Perhaps even then the seeds of that future desertion were there and his zeal was growing cold. There is not much to be said about him. He is just there. He is just Demas.

ॐ ॐ ॐ ॐ ॐ

15 Greet the brothers in Laodicea and also Nympha and the church in her house.
16 When this epistle has been read among you, have it *read* also in the church of *the* Laodiceans; and see that you read also the *one* from Laodicea.

Having sent along greetings from his companions, St. Paul then sends his own greetings to others, such as to the church in the neighboring city of **Laodicea**. He also tells the Colossians to pass along his letter to them to the church at Laodicea and to read the letter that was coming **from Laodicea**. Note that the letter coming was described not as "to the Laodiceans" but rather as **from Laodicea**. The letter in question is almost certainly the Epistle to the Ephesians, which was sent first to Ephesus, and then as a circular to all the churches of Asia Minor. It would seem as if this "Ephesian" epistle was coming to Colossae by way of Laodicea. Certainly, no genuine "Epistle to the Laodiceans" exists. The apostle almost certainly never wrote them a specific epistle. Rather, they received the "Ephesian" circular and then the Colossian epistle which was sent to them in exchange.

Also singled out for greetings was **Nympha and the church in her house**. (Some MSS read this as "Nymphas [a masculine name] and the church in their house," but the Greek *Nymphan* is almost certainly the accusative form of the feminine Nympha.) In Laodicea, there were perhaps a series of house churches, where the local subsets of the Christian community met. **Nympha** seems to have been one of the Christian women of that city who hosted the weekly meetings of the church. It is part of St. Paul's courtesy that he does not forget to thank those who graciously open their homes to the church.

ॐ ॐ ॐ ॐ ॐ

17 And say to Archippus, "Watch the ministry which you received in *the* Lord, that you fulfill it."

Last of all in his personal greetings, St. Paul has a word of encouragement to **Archippus**. He tells him to **watch the ministry** he received, to **fulfill it**. The word translated here *ministry* is the Greek word *diakonia*. It can mean simply "service" or "ministry" and not necessarily the ministerial diaconate per se. It could be that Archippus was not a deacon, but had some other unspecified form of church ministry—perhaps that of the presbyterate or some other task. Nonetheless, I would suggest that he was an actual ministerial deacon. In his letter to Philemon, St. Paul writes to "Philemon, Apphia our sister and to Archippus." It is most likely that Philemon was the head and presbyteral presider over one of the Colossian house churches, that Apphia was his wife, and Archippus was therefore their son. If this is so, it is quite likely that Archippus served his overseeing father as his deacon—much the same as sons of clergy today serve their fathers as altar boys. His diaconal work was challenging, perhaps because of his youth, perhaps because of difficulties at home. (Was Philemon perhaps a difficult and overbearing man and was it this difficulty that made the slave Onesimus run away? We can only speculate.) St. Paul's encouragement to Archippus needn't be taken to mean that he was slack in fulfilling his work and needed a rebuke; only that, for whatever reason, the work itself was challenging. (Later tradition would make Archippus pastor in neighboring Laodicea, finally dying a martyr. There is nothing improbable in this. Perhaps he later left home to take up residence in Laodicea and found himself providing overseeing leadership there as he provided diaconal service in Colossae.)

The tradition that would make him one of "the Seventy" disciples of Christ (see Luke 10:1) needs, however, to be handled with care. If Archippus were, say, 25 at the time of St. Paul's writing to Colossae, he would not yet have been born when our Lord sent out the Seventy. (For the age to work out properly, Archippus would have to have been about 62 years old at the time of St. Paul's writing Colossians, assuming him to have been our Lord's contemporary when He sent out the Seventy. That makes him a bit old to be receiving youthful encouragement as Philemon's son! In addition, the Seventy were Jews, and Archippus and his family obviously Gentiles. Archippus may be said to be "of the Seventy" in the sense that he was part of the apostolic first-century generation.)

§X   Concluding Blessing (4:18)

ॐ ॐ ॐ ॐ ॐ

18 The greeting of my *own* hand: of Paul. Remember my bonds. Grace be with you.

Finally St. Paul concludes with a word of attestation and his apostolic blessing. Epistles then were most often written by a secretary to whom the letter was orally dictated. It was St. Paul's custom to add his personal signature (**of Paul**) to his letters as proof of their authenticity (see 2 Thess. 3:17). Evidently, the apostle had an unusually unforgeable signature! Before his final blessing of **Grace be with you**, commending them to the Lord's grace and merciful care, he adds a final touching request: **Remember my bonds**. "Don't forget that I'm in prison," he poignantly adds. Though a mighty and far-famed apostle, the great man still humbly relies on the prayers of the nameless rank and file. The epistle thus ends on a note of vulnerability and grace.

❧ The Epistle of St. Paul the Apostle to Philemon ❧

Slavery in the Ancient World

"The slave," said Aristotle, "is a living tool and the tool a lifeless slave." That is, a slave was a thing and not a person. He or she had no legal rights whatsoever and was popularly thought to be inferior to a real person in every way—physically, mentally, and morally. It was held that slaves had their innate inferiority "hard-wired" into them—that certain men were destined to be slaves and servants of others. Slaves being cross-examined for legal matters were routinely tortured to ensure honesty. They could not marry, could be bought and sold (like any other object), and could be branded in the face if their master suspected they were planning escape. Runaway slaves, when apprehended, could be executed in the most brutal way then imagined, by crucifixion.

The condition of slaves ran the gamut, from the privileged slaves who were servants to the imperial household and who did the jobs now done by the civil service, to other slaves who worked the mines and whose condition was little more than an extended death sentence. In between, there were many others whose condition varied widely: slaves worked in temples, in agricultural fields, cared for and taught children, acted as business agents for their masters, and worked at trades or as physicians. As such, they constituted a sizable portion of the population. Indeed, it was considered that about twenty percent of the residents of Rome were slaves. (In Pergamum, the percentage was thought to be even higher—about thirty-three percent of the city's adult population.)

One could become a slave in a number of ways. One could be born a slave, or become one through selling oneself in payment of a debt. One could be condemned by the law court to become a slave or be captured through war or piracy.

One could at length be set free from slavery. One could save up one's wages and so purchase one's own freedom from a willing master, or one could be set free upon the master's death, if so stipulated in his will. Sometimes a slave was freed by his master on the condition that he continue to do some work for him, so that the master functioned as the patron of the freed man.

Slaves were considered by most as an indispensable part of society, and the average man simply could not picture a world where slavery did not exist. The first-century Church, for its part, did not indulge in radical social critique for which the world was not yet ready. To declare against slavery or otherwise encourage the slaves to rebel would have been disastrous. The rebellion itself would have been instantly crushed with the greatest possible brutality, and the Church would forever after have been labeled as seditious. This charge of inherent sedition was in fact just the charge against which St. Paul was defending himself in his prison in Rome!

Besides, the Church's task as the Body of the risen Christ was not to improve or tinker with the social system; it was to offer all men everywhere eternal life in the age to come. That is, its focus was eschatological. That did not mean that the Church was indifferent to human suffering—far from it. The Lord Himself placed the greatest importance on helping the poor and relieving their suffering (see Luke 12:33; 16:19–31). When the Church had the social means to do so, it built hospitals, orphanages, and leprosariums. Indeed, even during times of persecution when it was marginalized and powerless, it still fed the poor—so much so that the pagans complained that the Christians looked after not only their own poor, but those of everyone else as well!

Nonetheless, the main mandate of the Church was not social reform, but rather the proclamation of eternal life in the Kingdom of God. In the Church, the age to come had in fact appeared on earth in seminal and sacramental form, as a *musterion*. In Christ, the New Creation, the New Humanity, had appeared—a humanity in which all former categories and divisions were transcended. Not only the categories of Jew and Gentile, but of slave and free as well. The Kingdom thus transvalued all the arithmetic of this age, giving to all earthly things a new value. Thus, in Christ, it did not ultimately matter whether one were slave or free. The slave was truly free in Christ, and the free man was the Lord's slave (1 Cor. 7:22). All social distinctions of this age would pass away along with this age, giving place to joy in the Kingdom of God. The heart's cry of the Church was not, "Improve the world!" but rather, "Let grace come and let the world pass away!" (Didache 10). In this context, freedom and slavery could have only a relative value.

Onesimus

Onesimus was a slave living in Colossae, owned by Philemon, who was himself patron (and probably presbyter-overseer) of one of its house churches. For some reason, whether because of the perceived harshness of his master, or from youthful impatience and rebellion, or from some other unknown impulse, he decided he had had enough of it all. He stole a sum of money from his master's household and fled the city, taking refuge in the teeming anonymity of a great metropolis. That is, he found himself at length in Rome. He was then a wanted criminal and he knew it. He would have been quite aware of what savagery the law reserved for runaways like himself. If apprehended as a fugitive slave, he could be branded on his face with the letter "F" (for fugitivis), or crucified, or both. Whatever happiness or misery now awaited him, he had "burned his bridges." There could be no going back.

We do not know how long he was in Rome, or what contacts (if any) he had there, or what adventures befell him. We do know that eventually he became a Christian there. The Christian Faith must have been immensely attractive to slaves like him. In a world where all (especially slaves) were powerless before cosmic forces, entangled and caught in the cords of control by a multitude of gods and other powers, the Christians offered a way of escape. Christian baptism offered a liberation from all the sorrows of this age, freely and effectively, without any regard for a person's race or social standing. A slave like Onesimus could scarcely dream of becoming a Roman citizen, yet here was freely offered the superior status of becoming a son and heir of God! No wonder that he responded to such a message!

And not only he, but many other slaves as well. (So many, in fact, that a pagan opponent of the Church, Celsus by name, wrote derisively, "Hear what kind of folk these Christians call! 'Whoever is a sinner,' they say, 'whoever is unwise, whoever is a child, and in a word, whoever is a wretch, the Kingdom of God will receive him!'" As Celsus bears reluctant witness, the Church apparently had great success indeed in calling the humble of the earth home to salvation.)

We can only speculate how Onesimus came to the Faith and by what path. Perhaps it was through his Colossian contacts in Rome that he met Epaphras, who was a Colossian himself (see Col. 4:12). If this were so, not only would Onesimus have learned about Christ, but Epaphras would also have learned about Onesimus. At length it seems that the runaway slave told his story to the church there, as he presented himself as a candidate for baptism. There could be no hiding the truth.

If this was so, and Epaphras was the one who received his story, it only made sense for Epaphras to introduce Onesimus to St. Paul in prison, since St. Paul was personally acquainted with Onesimus's old master, Philemon. Certainly, it was clearly impossible for the church there to be harboring a runaway slave—this would have endangered them all. There was nothing for it: Onesimus the runaway would have to return home. It was here that St. Paul's contact and friendship with Philemon became crucial. Onesimus could accompany St. Paul's friend Tychicus on his journey to Asia Minor, where he was going to deliver epistles to the Ephesians (probably as a circular for the entire area) and to the Colossians. He could also deliver a letter from St. Paul to Philemon at the same time and help vouch for Onesimus.

So it was that the Epistle of St. Paul the Apostle to Philemon was written, the only purely personal letter in the New Testament. It was written to smooth the way for Onesimus to return to Philemon's household. For it took a great deal of courage for Onesimus to return home. This return was not only immensely awkward, but (as we have seen) potentially fatal. St. Paul's letter was an appeal for him to be forgiven, restored, and integrated into the church over which Philemon in part presided.

The Lasting Significance of the Epistle

If St. Paul's letter to his friend Philemon were of only individual significance, it would be a bit mysterious why the Church included it in the New Testament canon, for then it would have no more importance than the apostle's shopping list or other purely personal matters. But in fact it has a wider and more abiding meaning for the Church at large. Its significance is twofold, both ascetic and social.

The epistle's *ascetic* significance lies in the fact that it is an illustration of the nature of Christian repentance and reconciliation. It would have been easy for Onesimus to deny his past, to pretend his disloyal desertion of his master had never occurred, and to proceed with the rest of his life as a Christian. But one cannot build a life of devotion to the Truth on the foundation of a lie. If he had really repented of his sins, he must return to Philemon to make restitution. St. Paul sent him back, not only because to harbor a runaway slave would have been to endanger them all. It was also for the sake of Onesimus's salvation. For there can be no true reconciliation with God that is not also simultaneously reconciliation with one's neighbor.

The greater abiding significance of the epistle lies in its *social* implications. For St. Paul sent Onesimus back home not just to restore the status quo. He was not returned merely as a repentant slave, but now as a brother in Christ (see Philemon 16). That is, it must be recognized that he was not a thing, but a person. This insight completely undercut the philosophical foundation of slavery, which asserted that slaves were things to be bought and sold, and not persons to be loved and respected. Onesimus now would share with his master the eucharistic chalice of the Blood of Christ—that Blood which had been shed equally for him, the slave, as for his free master. Together they were offered the same reward of the inheritance of eternal life as the sons of God—and, as the sons of God, they found that they were therefore brothers. The integration of Onesimus into the Christian community of Colossae was a pledge of the eventual doom of slavery as an institution. For it was apparent to all that the Christians did not really believe in slavery. To them, slaves were not "things" or living tools, but potential sons and heirs of God. The Epistle to Philemon was the handwriting on the wall for slavery in the Roman Empire. If the Christians' principles were ever to be put into full social effect, slavery would be no more.

❧ The Epistle to Philemon ❧

§I   Opening Greetings (1–3)

> ॐ ॐ ॐ ॐ ॐ
>
> 1 Paul, a prisoner of Christ Jesus, and Timothy
> the brother, to Philemon our beloved and
> co-worker,
> 2 and to Apphia the sister, and to Archippus our
> co-soldier, and to the church in your house:
> 3 Grace to you and peace from God our Father
> and the Lord Jesus Christ.

The apostle does not begin with a formal assertion of his apostolic authority (as was customary in his epistles to churches, e.g. Col. 1:1). Rather, he describes himself merely as the humble **prisoner of Christ Jesus.** That is, though ostensibly the prisoner of Rome, he is in fact under the care of the Lord, for whom he suffers this imprisonment. With this self-description, he sets the tone for the rest of the letter—not one of formal giving of orders, but a heartfelt appeal from one who suffers (and who thus has the moral right to make such appeals; see vv. 8, 9). As is usual, he includes his **brother** in Christ **Timothy** with him in his writing. The apostle was never a loner, but worked as part of a collegial team, even in such personal matters as this.

Since this is a household matter, he writes not only to **Philemon** but also to all in the household, including Philemon's wife, **Apphia**, and their son, **Archippus**. In his form of address, the apostle again reveals his warm affection for them. Philemon is **beloved** of St. Paul and he respects him as his **co-worker** and colleague in apostolic labors. His wife is described, with the formality and respect due a married woman, simply as Paul's **sister** (i.e. omitting the description "beloved"). Their son **Archippus** is not patronized, but described as the apostle's **co-soldier**. As suggested above in the Commentary to the Colossians, Archippus seems to have been a deacon in the church there, serving his clerical father. (If this was not the case, it is apparent that Philemon at least hosted the church, opening his home for holding church services, even if he was not a presbyter-bishop. And if Archippus was not an actual deacon, he evidently held some official position of leadership and prominence.)

Also addressed is **the church in your house**. By including the entire house church in this personal matter, St. Paul reveals that there are few purely private matters when it comes to one's own faith and Christian duty. What affects Philemon affects them all (especially if he was one of the Colossian presbyter-bishops). It is of concern to the church as well that they might soon have in their sacramental midst a new brother—one who was formerly a fugitive slave!

§II   Opening Thanksgiving (4–7)

4   I give thanks to my God always, making remembrance of you in my prayers,
5   because I hear of your love and of the faith which you have toward the Lord Jesus and all the saints;
6   and I pray that the sharing of your faith may become effective through the real-knowledge of every good *thing* that is in you for Christ's sake.
7   For I have come to have much joy and encouragement from your love, for the inner-*hearts* of the saints have been refreshed through you, brother.

As was customary in those days, St. Paul begins his letter with thanksgiving and prayer. He assures Philemon that he always prays for him, **giving thanks** to God, and that Philemon is a source of joy to him. He finds Philemon a joy to his heart because of Philemon's

love and **faith**. Philemon is pious and devout before the Lord, and he shows this by letting this devotion flow out to **all the saints**. As one would expect from someone who opens his home to the local church at large, Philemon has a keen sense of the responsibilities of love. St. Paul's prayer for him, therefore, is that he continue in this good way. He prays that Philemon may continue to let **the sharing** [Gr. *koinonia*] **of** his **faith become effective** in others, so that they may come to experience and have **real-knowledge** [Gr. *epignosis*] **of every good** *thing* **that is in** them **for Christ's sake**. That is, he prays that as Philemon shares his faith with those around him, this may cause true and intimate knowledge of all the blessings of Christ to become effective and active in their lives.

This is consistent with the Philemon that he has come to know. St. Paul assures him that he himself has had **much joy and encouragement from your love**, as many others have had also. Indeed, he writes, **the inner-*hearts*** [Gr. *splagchna*] **of the saints have been refreshed through you**. The word *splagchna* (translated here with some awkwardness as *inner-hearts*) is difficult to put here into elegant and proper English. It literally means "bowels," "innards," affections, inmost selves (see its use in Phil. 1:8; 2:1). Similarly, the word translated *refreshed* (Gr. *anapauo*) means "to rest" (see its use in Mark 6:31, where the Lord urged His disciples to come apart and "rest" a little, since they were too busy even to eat). What the apostle means here is that Philemon has given rest and refreshment to the true believers in their inmost selves, strengthening them from deep within, putting a new heart and vigor into them. He is that kind of person—giving generously of himself to strengthen and encourage all those around him. No wonder St. Paul addresses him as **brother**— that is, with the hearty affection due a close family member.

§III   Appeal for Onesimus (8–22)

༈ ༈ ༈ ༈ ༈

8   **Therefore, though I have much boldness in Christ to command you** *to do* **what is fitting,**

> 9 yet because of *our* love, I rather encourage
> you—since I am such a one as Paul, the elder,
> and now also a prisoner of Christ Jesus—
> 10 I encourage you for my child whom I have
> begotten in my bonds, Onesimus,

The apostle comes at last to the reason for writing the letter—though perhaps by now Philemon could guess, since the former fugitive Onesimus accompanied Tychicus, the bearer of the letter! That is, he appeals on behalf of his slave Onesimus. The **therefore** is significant: "Because you are so generous to all," St. Paul writes, "*therefore* I am bold to make this request." By stressing how generous he is (vv. 4–7), the apostle makes it difficult for Philemon to deny him his request.

The request is for Onesimus, whom he describes as **my child whom I have begotten in my bonds** (that is, while in prison). The slave is not simply one for whom the apostle is writing an impersonal "To Whom It May Concern" letter of reference. On the contrary, St. Paul considers him to be his spiritual child, **begotten** by him while in prison. Whether this means that St. Paul actually was the one who finally converted Onesimus or whether he speaks of the ongoing relation of father to spiritual son, he means to indicate a great closeness now existing between them. Indeed, in sending back Onesimus, he is sending his very "inner-heart" (v. 12; Gr. *splagchna*, see its use in v. 7).

Note the skill and diplomatic delicacy with which St. Paul undertakes this appeal. He begins by bringing in the weight of his apostolic authority (with which he could **command** him *to do what is fitting*), but says that he is not using it! (But don't let Philemon forget that he could!) Rather, St. Paul **encourages** him to do the right and fitting thing **because of** their **love**. How could Philemon deny him his request—since he was **Paul, the elder** (Gr. *presbutes*), a poor old man (perhaps actually only 55 or so, but aged by suffering), and one languishing as a **prisoner of Christ** besides!

It is not until he has well paved the way for his actual request

that St. Paul mentions what the request is and writes the unwel-
come name of **Onesimus**. In the Greek text, the name Onesimus is
kept to the very end of the sentence! And not just "Onesimus," but
my child Onesimus! St. Paul leaves no doubt as to the affection
that binds the runaway slave to his apostolic heart.

ॐ ॐ ॐ ॐ ॐ

11 the one once useless to you, but now useful
both to you and to me.
12 I am sending him back to you, that is, *sending
back* my inner-*heart*,
13 whom I *myself* desired to hold back with me,
so that on your behalf he might serve me in
my bonds *for the sake of preaching of* the
Gospel;
14 but I willed to do nothing apart from your
consent, so that your good would not be as
from necessity but voluntarily.

In making his appeal, he emphasizes how much Onesimus has
changed. Formerly he was **useless** (Gr. *achrestos*), but now he is a
changed man and truly **useful** (Gr. *euchrestos*)—to Philemon, of
course, but to Paul as well. Here St. Paul breaks the tension of an
awkward moment by injecting a bit of humor, for the name
"Onesimus" means "useful." He used to be quite useless, granted!
But no more! Now he is truly useful and a good man to have around.
So useful, in fact, that the apostle would have liked to keep him
there with him, keeping a tight hold on such a good man, who
could **serve** him on Philemon's behalf and help him in his *preaching of* the Gospel. (The word translated *hold back*, Gr. *katecho*,
means "to restrain, hold tight"; see its use in 2 Thess. 2:6. The word
suggests that St. Paul was quite reluctant to let Onesimus go.) But
he determined not to do any such thing without Philemon's express
permission and decision. For such a **good** work as letting Onesimus
stay in Rome should come **voluntarily**, not as if it were **from**

necessity, with Philemon having no choice in the matter. By stressing how much he wanted to keep him there with him, St. Paul lets Philemon know what a changed man Onesimus now is—and therefore (more to the point) what an asset he would be to Philemon at home!

ॐ ॐ ॐ ॐ ॐ

15 **For perhaps because of this he was separated** *from you* **for a moment, that you would receive him** *back* **forever,**

16 **no longer as a slave, but more than a slave, as a beloved brother, especially to me, but how much more to you, both in** *the* **flesh and in** *the* **Lord.**

The apostle continues his appeal. He suggests tentatively that perhaps, in the Providence of God, that is why Onesimus was **separated** from Philemon for a time in the first place—so that he could be converted and Philemon could have him back permanently as a brother in Christ. (Note too how carefully the apostle chooses his words. He does not say, "Perhaps that's why he *ran away*," but instead, "Perhaps that's why he **was separated** *from you*"—a more diplomatic way of describing his theft and flight!) Now that he is back, though, he will be back **forever** (Gr. *aionion*, "eternally, to the ages"). There will be no more running away. And he is back, not just as a slave, but now as **more than a slave**—as **a beloved brother**. He is **beloved** of St. Paul, of course, but (the apostle insists) beloved of Philemon as well! In fact there will now be a double bond binding Onesimus to the household: both the bond **in** *the* **flesh** (that is, of his slavery) and also **in** *the* **Lord** (that is, of his new Christian Faith).

ॐ ॐ ॐ ॐ ॐ

17 **If then you hold me as a sharer** *in your work*, **accept him as** *you would* **me.**

> 18 But if *in* anything he has wronged you or owes
>   *you*, charge that to my account.
> 19 I *myself*, Paul, write this with my *own* hand: *it
>   is* I *who* will repay! (not to say to you that you
>   owe to me even your *own* self as well).

St. Paul then concludes his appeal with something rather like an order: **If then you hold me as a sharer** in the work of faith (Gr. *koinonos*), **accept him** as you would accept me. To show how emotionally involved he is in this, St. Paul puts himself and his money on the line. **If . . . he has wronged you or owes *you*** anything (that is, if you are concerned for what he stole when he fled), then you may **charge that to my account**. He even signs it himself: **I *myself*, Paul, write this with my *own* hand**, as a legally binding contract. *It is* **I *who* will repay!** (The **I** is emphatic in the Greek.) This is not to bring up the matter, says St. Paul—bringing up the matter!—that Philemon **owes** him his *own* **self** as well!

How St. Paul met Philemon and in what way Philemon was morally indebted to him, we do not know. Perhaps it was when St. Paul was preaching for two years a hundred miles away in Ephesus, when "all in Asia heard the Word" (Acts 19:10). Certainly, Philemon did feel himself indebted to the apostle, and it is this debt that the apostle is "calling in," and that in a none-too-subtle way. Certainly Philemon has no real room to maneuver or refuse the request. To bring the appeal down to a matter of money and to sign an IOU for Onesimus's debts—and on top of that, to remind Philemon of his underlying moral debt to St. Paul—is something of an overkill. But the apostle speaks from the fullness of his heart and out of concern for his poor trembling young friend Onesimus. He is therefore leaving nothing to chance.

> ॐ ॐ ॐ ॐ ॐ
> 20 Yes, brother, I myself would have some use from
>   you in the Lord; refresh my inner-heart in Christ.

He concludes by trying to lighten the mood (made quite heavy by his last three sentences). He inserts another joke, a typically Jewish one, making a pun on the name "Onesimus" and saying, **Yes, brother, I** *myself* **would have some use from you in** *the* **Lord**—the word **use** (Gr. *onaimen*) being a pun on the name Onesimus, "useful." It is meant to reset the tone of brotherly affection established earlier—hence the repetition of the warm and intimate address of Philemon as **brother** (see v. 7). One can almost see the apostle hitting Philemon playfully on the shoulder, saying, "C'mon, dear brother, give me a break!" And then, as the love from his great heart bursts out, he adds, **refresh my inner-***heart* **in Christ**! These are the same words which he earlier used to describe Philemon: he always gives the apostle so much joy and love because it is always his way to "refresh the inner-hearts of the saints" by his love and generosity (v. 7). Do it again, St. Paul urges. You were always the one whose love strengthened the hearts of God's people. Do this again for me!

ॐ ॐ ॐ ॐ ॐ

21 Being persuaded of your obedience, I write to you, knowing that you will do even more than what I say.

Having made his appeal with all his strength, he leaves it with Philemon (and Tychicus, the bearer of the letter, who can be depended upon to add more entreaties if it proves necessary!). As a final touch, he says that he is **persuaded** and confident that Philemon will respond with **obedience** (not that it's an order or anything!). And he **knows** that Philemon will **do even more** than what is asked. What is this unstated **even more**? The most obvious guess is that St. Paul refers to setting Onesimus free. That would truly be a worthy crown and culmination of their reconciliation in Christ and an image of the overflowing grace of God. To return home fearing punishment and to be greeted, not only with the hoped-for forgiveness, but also with the liberation for which he dared not hope! That would be a Christian homecoming indeed! It is as if the suggestion trembles on the lip of the apostle, who dares not utter it. For this above all cannot come as obedience to an apostolic order—even an unstated one. To be truly an image and manifestation of God's grace, it must come straight from the heart of Philemon, as unbidden and unexpected as possible.

ॐ ॐ ॐ ॐ ॐ

22 At the same time also prepare me a guest room, for I hope that through your prayers I will be given to you.

St. Paul turns his attention to other things as he closes. He hopes to be acquitted and released **through** their **prayers** and **given to** them (Gr. *charitoo*; see its use in Phil. 1:29). That is, he hopes that God will graciously grant that he be set free. That being the case, he hopes to come and visit them while passing through Colossae and will need a **guest room** with them for a brief time. He thus ends on this note of happy optimism, anticipating their joyful reunion after his release.

§IV   Final Greetings (23, 24)

ॐ ॐ ॐ ॐ ॐ

23 Epaphras, my co-captive in Christ Jesus, greets you,
24 as do Mark, Aristarchus, Demas, Luke, my co-workers.

As is customary with letters of that time, final greetings are added. **Epaphras**, as the founder of the Colossian church, heads the list; St. Paul describes him with a light touch as his **co-captive**, since he shares so much of his time in prison. Also sending greetings are **Mark, Aristarchus, Demas,** and **Luke.** They are briefly described as his colleagues in the apostolic work of preaching, his **co-workers.**

They are also present in the conclusion of the Epistle to the Colossians, where they are described (along with others) in greater detail. Here they are therefore simply mentioned in passing.

§V   Concluding Blessing (25)

ॐ ॐ ॐ ॐ ॐ

25 The grace of the Lord Jesus Christ be with your spirit.

As in all his letters, St. Paul leaves them with a blessing, solemnly invoking the **grace of the Lord Jesus Christ** upon their inner hearts and **spirit**.

A Postscript:
Onesimus in Later Church History

It seems beyond all reasonable doubt that Philemon did indeed welcome the runaway home and integrate him as a brother into the church in his house (v. 2). It is not unreasonable to suggest that he also granted Onesimus his freedom.

What later become of this Onesimus? We cannot know for sure. But there are several traditions in later church history. One is that Onesimus became bishop in Berea in Macedonia (Apostolic Constitutions, Book 7, chapter 46). Another is that he became bishop of Ephesus in Asia Minor (for the bishop of Ephesus in the time of St. Ignatius' martyrdom in 107 had the name of Onesimus—see Ignatius' Letter to the Ephesians, chapter 1—but it was not an uncommon name). Some say that he was eventually martyred in Rome, and others that he was martyred in Puteoli. Whatever the historical specifics, we may rejoice in his faith and the work that he did for the Kingdom. He was enrolled with all the saints (his feast day is February 15) and has received his heavenly reward. The lonely slave, trembling and fugitive in a vast foreign city, has at last come truly and eternally home.

About the Author

Archpriest Lawrence Farley currently pastors St. Herman of Alaska Orthodox Mission (OCA) in Surrey, B.C., Canada. He received his B.A. from Trinity College, Toronto, and his M.Div. from Wycliffe College, Toronto. A former Anglican priest, he converted to Orthodoxy in 1985 and studied for two years at St. Tikhon's Orthodox Seminary in Pennsylvania. He has also published *Let Us Attend: A Journey Through the Orthodox Divine Liturgy.*

Visit www.ancientfaithradio.com to listen to Fr. Lawrence Farley's regular podcast, "The Coffee Cup Commentaries."

Also in the
Orthodox Bible Study Companion Series

The Gospel of Matthew: Torah for the Church
400 pages (ISBN 978-0-9822770-7-2) CP Order No. 007728—$22.95*

The Gospel of Mark: The Suffering Servant
224 pages (ISBN 978-1-888212-54-9) CP Order No. 006035—$16.95*

The Gospel of Luke: Good News for the Poor
432 pages (ISBN 978-1-936270-12-5) CP Order No. 008106—$24.95*

The Gospel of John: Beholding the Glory
376 pages (ISBN 978-1-888212-55-6) CP Order No. 007110—$19.95*

The Epistle to the Romans: A Gospel for All
208 pages (ISBN 978-1-888212-51-8) CP Order No. 005675—$15.95*

First and Second Corinthians: Straight from the Heart
319 pages (ISBN 9781-888212-53-2) CP Order No. 006129—$17.95*

Words of Fire: The Early Epistles of Saint Paul to the Thessalonians and the Galatians
168 pages (ISBN 978-1-936270-02-6) CP Order No. 008029 —$ 15.95*

Shepherding the Flock: The Pastoral Epistles of Saint Paul the Apostle to Timothy and Titus
144 pages (ISBN 978-1-888212-56-3) CP Order No. 007516—$13.95*

Universal Truth: The Catholic Epistles of James, Peter, Jude and John
232 pages (ISBN 978-1-888212-60-0) CP Order No. 007611—$15.95*

*plus applicable tax and postage & handling charges. Prices current as of 5/2011. Please call Conciliar Press at 800-967-7377 for complete ordering information. Check our website (www.conciliarpress.com) for announcements of future releases in this series.

Conciliar Media Ministries hopes you have enjoyed and benefited from this book. The proceeds from the sales of our books only partially cover the costs of operating our nonprofit ministry—which includes both the work of **Conciliar Press** and the work of **Ancient Faith Radio.** Your financial support makes it possible to continue this ministry both in print and online. Donations are tax-deductible and can be made at www.ancientfaith.com.

ANCIENT FAITH RADIO

Internet-Based Orthodox Radio:
Podcasts, 24-hour music and talk stations,
teaching, conference recordings, and much more,
at www.ancientfaith.com

CPSIA information can be obtained at www.ICGtesting.com
Printed in the USA
LVOW05s0534120314

377061LV00002B/8/P